GO

Other Abingdon Press Books by George G. Hunter III

Should We Change Our Game Plan?

The Celtic Way of Evangelism

The Apostolic Congregation

Leading and Managing a Growing Church

GO

The Church's Main Purpose

George G. Hunter III

Foreword by Bishop Mike Lowry

Abingdon Press
Nashville

GO:
THE CHURCH'S MAIN PURPOSE

Copyright © 2017 by Abingdon Press

This book is printed on acid-free paper.

Library of Congress Cataloging-in-Publication Data has been requested.

ISBN: 978-1-5018-3549-0

Unless otherwise indicated, all scripture quotations are from the Common English Bible. Copyright © 2011 by the Common English Bible. All rights reserved. Used by permission. www.CommonEnglishBible.com.

Scripture quotations marked KJV are from The Authorized (King James) Version. Rights in the Authorized Version in the United Kingdom are vested in the Crown. Reproduced by permission of the Crown's patentee, Cambridge University Press.

Leading & Managing a Growing Church, Copyright © 2000 by Abingdon Press. Used by permission. All rights reserved.

17 18 19 20 21 22 23 24 25 26—10 9 8 7 6 5 4 3 2 1
MANUFACTURED IN THE UNITED STATES OF AMERICA

To the memory of
Kermit Long,
George Krumme,
and Sollie McCreless

Contents

Contents

Contents

Foreword

L egend has it that when Mother Teresa visited America in the mid-1980s, she was interviewed by a reporter after one presentation. The reporter allegedly asked her what she thought of the United States. This great saint, who poured her life out in the streets of Calcutta, feeding the hungry, sheltering the homeless, and caring for the dying, is said to have replied, "I've never seen a people so hungry."

We live in a time of great spiritual hunger. The angst of our culture demonstrates almost a frenetic spiritual searching. While many are leaving the old "mainline" churches and religious attendance in Sunday worship continues on a steady decline, spiritual seeking counterintuitively continues on a steady climb. The almost nonsensical phrase "spiritual but not religious" has ensconced itself deeply in the culture of the North American mission field.

Amid this cultural backdrop, Christian churches and denominations struggle to find their footing. In a long and distinguished career as pastor, professor, denominational executive, and seminary dean, George Hunter has been at the forefront of the battle to recover viable evangelism in the Wesleyan tradition. In *Go: The Church's Main Purpose* he champions a desperately needed recovery of the heart and soul, the main purpose of the church as a mission post of the advancing kingdom of God. Without apology Dr. Hunter anchors his argument both biblically (Matthew 28:16-20) and historically in the call and claim of Christ on faithful Christians in faithful churches. He gifts the church with a concise understanding of the church's main purpose: "A church's *mission*, locally and globally, is its main business (or should be). The 'real church' is an *ecclesia*—the 'called out' people of God whom the Lord shapes into an *apostolate*, then 'sends out' to be publicly present in the world, but not of the world. The mission is serving, witnessing, inviting outreach to all people—in their many tribes and affinity groups."

To people, churches, and cultures with a deep spiritual hunger he offers hope through a recovery of following in the way of Christ. In offering hope to a struggling and confused church, Dr. Hunter challenges us to reappropriate seminal insights of the New Testament gospels. Using the Gospel of Luke as a model, he demonstrates how our Lord teaches us to offer the way of life in his name. In a real sense, with concrete practical examples and applications, the author challenges us to "go back to the future."

Using two concrete, exceptionally practical examples of application, Dr. Hunter invites the reader to discover (or rediscover) essential sociological and cultural insights grained through modern research in affinity groups and reaching across cultural, social, and ethnic barriers to a more holistic and spiritually faithful church. In doing so he debunks the insights of Natural Church Development and offers a far more nuanced and faithful version for how to grow the church through adding disciples.

In this powerful writing we gain the benefits, insights, and technical research of decades of study in communication and leadership to the end that people might come to put their allegiance in Christ as Lord and engage with the church as expressions of the outreaching and upwardly reaching body of Christ. Don't read this book if you don't want to be challenged. Wrestle deeply with Hunter's research, insights, and proposal for the future if you wish to be engaged in living out the future in a world consumed by a great cultural emptiness and desperate spiritual hunger. In these pages, hunger meets hope and is offered help—in the name of the Lord.

Bishop Mike Lowry
Resident Bishop of the Fort Worth Episcopal Area,
The Central Texas Conference of the United Methodist Church,
Fort Worth, TX

Preface

In the early 1900s, two small companies in Detroit, the Ace Buggy Whip Company and the Ford Transportation Company, were serving the nation's drivers of horse-drawn vehicles. Each company manufactured whips, springs, luggage racks, through-braces, and other products used in the era when some people still traveled by foot, bicycle, or horseback, but more and more people rode in horse-drawn carts, buggies, carriages, covered wagons, and stagecoaches.

The steam engine was the revolutionary technological innovation of the era. Larger numbers of people could travel faster and farther by steam-powered trams, trains, and ships like the *Titanic*. Steam engines had already powered the new factories that catalyzed the industrial revolution and the expansion of cities. The science fiction of Jules Verne, Mary Shelley, and H. G. Wells inspired the reading public to imagine that steam would one day power computers and flying machines and transport people into space. The "steampunk" era is still a fount of nostalgia.

Meanwhile in Germany, Karl Benz crafted the first gasoline-powered "internal combustion" automobile. The first "motor cars" were so expensive that few people could afford one, but interest in cars grew. Urban legend tells us that Ace perceived the mounting interest in cars as a threat. They joined forces with other companies in the carriage industry and charged that cars were loud, foul smelling, and dangerous. They lobbied the government to save the nation's economy by outlawing automobiles.

Henry Ford also perceived the shift in public interest—not as a threat, however, but as an opportunity; so he started making cars. For several years, he could produce only a few cars per day, and they were still expensive. Then Ford conceived of the assembly line and learned how to manage a large workforce, and reasonably priced cars were possible. In 1908, the first Ford Model T rolled off of the assembly line; soon, Ford was selling millions of them and the rest, as they say, is history.

In some ways the two companies, Ace and Ford, were once similar; they both manufactured buggy whips and related products. They differed, however, in one supremely important way: how they defined their "main business." The Ace people defined their main business as making such things as buggy whips. The Ford people defined their main business as facilitating personal transportation. In time, Ace died and Ford thrived. Their diverging histories were rooted in that one difference.

"What is your main business?" Peter Drucker, the supreme guru of the twentieth century's revolution in leadership and management lore, advised the leaders of organizations, especially nonprofit organizations, to ask that question often.

The answer that drives many organizations is less than clear; presumably they used to be clear, but gradually they forgot, or they changed their mind, or they let others change it for them.

Take universities for instance. The institutions were once clear that their main business was to educate students and advance knowledge. That is reasonably clear: one mission, two core objectives. But many colleges and universities now seem driven by some contrasting *priority* agenda—such as preparing students for careers; or moving up in the rankings; or achieving diversity; or pleasing accrediting agencies; or becoming high-tech; or proliferating procedures, meetings, and vice presidents; or winning basketball games.

The University of Kentucky, near where I live, claims "the greatest tradition in the history of college basketball." Almost no one around here seems to care that a bellwether state university is best known, worldwide, for its basketball team; almost no one seems to notice when knowledge leadership is subordinated to athletic success. To his credit, our Hall-of-Fame coach does not even pretend that his best players are there primarily for an education; the faster they graduate to the NBA, the greater the program!

In the spirit of full disclosure, I am part of the problem. I share fully in the excitement when a UK player makes a shot from "downtown" or takes the ball "coast to coast!" When I recently opened an address in a church in Sacramento, I reported, "We sent you DeMarcus Cousins." (Laughter, applause, pause.) "You are welcome."

Now, you knew where I was headed with this. Churches can be similarly stricken.

I have lived and observed long enough, and have studied enough history, to know that whole denominations can lose their way, or forget their main business, or change their minds, or get hijacked by new leaders or coalitions who "know better." In time, their people are afflicted with amnesia.

Denominations often appear to "settle" for a primary objective that is less than the apostles would have recommended, like preserving the liturgy, music, tradition, polity, building, cemetery, or family values; or being trendy or ecumenical; or advancing diversity or clergy careers; or policing offensive language; or passing resolutions; or becoming wholly owned subsidiaries of one of the political parties at prayer. Their people, and their visitors, may wonder if "this is all there is to it."

Such denominations are traveling the Ace buggy whip path.

The more effective denominations and Christian movements, however, remember their main business. They adapt to their changing community, and they often refine their understanding of their main business. I teach and write books in the conviction that denominations that have settled, or have lost their way, can choose to recover an appropriate version of Christianity's "first love" and work for a very desirable future; if a denomination refuses, movements within it can flourish.

This book, however, focuses on local churches and local Christianity. I have observed, for a long time, that the leaders of most floundering or declining churches are not at all clear about their core driving purpose. Or some of the leaders have some answers—but no consensus. In more recent years, as the postmodern mood becomes more entrenched, I have observed that more and more leader groups now assume that they get to *decide* what Christianity's main business *should* be. After all, postmodern people are entitled to redefine anything they want to!

This book's honest bias is that Christianity's truth and its main business have been revealed. As we are the stewards of "the faith which was once delivered unto the saints" (Jude 1:3 KJV), so we are the heirs of the mission once entrusted to the apostles and their movements. I must not say much about that now—I'll save it for the first chapter and beyond—because I am told that most people do not bother reading a book's preface or introduction: they go straight to the first chapter!

Oh all right, since *you* have read the preface, I will let you in on it. (I have not made anything up; I, with others, have reflected from the very earliest phase of the Christian movement.) The book develops proposals that I have summarized in three sentences:

A church's *mission*, locally and globally, is its main business (or should be). The "real church" is an *ecclesia*—the "called out" people of God whom the Lord shapes into an *apostolate*, then

**"sends out" to be publicly present in the world, but not of the
world. This mission is a serving, witnessing, inviting outreach to
all people—in their many tribes and affinity groups.**

Each of those three sentences is the mere tip of an iceberg. Or,
to vary the analogy, there is much more gold in the three mountains
than one might guess; this includes readers who might assume they
already understand the three sentences.

This book's focus is consistent with several of my books that
unpack some of what is known about what a church's main business
might look like in secular Western societies—especially *How to Reach
Secular People, The Celtic Way of Evangelism, The Recovery of a Contagious Methodist Movement,* and *Should We Change Our Game Plan?*[1]

This book, like *To Spread the Power, Radical Outreach,* and *The
Apostolic Congregation,* focuses largely on how the churches might
fulfill their calling in *any* field of mission, including the secular (and
increasingly postmodern) West.[2]

Readers of my other books will notice that this book is com-
paratively thin on specific approaches, ministries, and methods that
churches can follow. This is because the first question needs to be
asked first once again. When a church becomes clear about its main
business and priority objectives, the "how" question then becomes
necessary.

But not always. Herb Miller, a popular seminar leader in the
Christian Church/Disciples of Christ tradition, used to ask audi-
ences, "How many of you can remember your first serious kiss?"
(Most people laughed and raised a hand.) "How many of you really

---

1. *How to Reach Secular People* (Nashville: Abingdon Press, 1992); *The Celtic
Way of Evangelism* (Nashville: Abingdon Press, 2000, rev. ed. 2010); *The Recovery
of a Contagious Methodist Movement* (Nashville: Abingdon Press, 2011); *Should We
Change Our Game Plan?* (Nashville: Abingdon Press, 2013).

2. *To Spread the Power* (Nashville: Abingdon Press, 1987); *Radical Outreach*
(Nashville: Abingdon Press, 2003); *The Apostolic Congregation* (Nashville: Abingdon
Press, 2009).

knew what you were doing?" (Few hands were raised). "To those of you who did not really know what you were doing, did that stop you?"

Sometimes, love just finds a way!

I have reached an age when I never know whether my latest book will be my last. So let me express gratitude for the privilege of spending a lifetime in ministry, research, field observation, teaching, and writing. I have dedicated this book to three devoted men who once made it possible for me to do doctoral studies and to begin my specialized quest to rethink, teach, and commend in writing what I have come to call *apostolic ministry*. The first found the funds, the second gave the funds, the third funded my first academic chair.

Chapter One

"What Is Your Main Business?"

I n the 1980s, a California megachurch raised a million dollars, apparently with the purpose of investing the money. The famous pastor telephoned the White House to speak to the distinguished economist Milton Friedman, who served on President Reagan's Council of Economic Advisers. When the pastor asked to speak to "Mr. Friedman," the White House switchboard connected the call to a speechwriter named Friedman. Urban legend reports the following conversation.

The pastor asked, "Mr. Friedman, how can our church strategically invest a million dollars?" The speechwriter replied, "Why don't you invest it in ministries for struggling people?" After a long silence, the pastor asked, "Sir, am I speaking to the real Milton Friedman?" The speechwriter replied, "Sir, are you calling from a real church?"

It may be time for leaders from almost every church, everywhere, to ask that question of their churches. Peter Drucker, the guru of the twentieth-century revolution in management theory, commented that there are two questions that the leaders of all organizations, especially organizations in the nonprofit sector (including churches),

1

need to ask frequently: (1) "What is our main business?" and (2) "How is business?"

I discovered Drucker's first question many years ago. I suppose I have asked, "What is your church's main business?" to the leaders of every church that I have researched, consulted with, or led training for ever since. The question is enormously useful in studying churches. The leaders usually have one or more articulate answers to the question. (Of course, when the leaders give a range of different answers, they discover that they might not be on the same page!)

I sometimes tested their answer to see the extent to which they practiced what they preach. I studied their budget, how they invested time, how they deployed staff, and especially how they deployed lay volunteers in service and ministry. For more subjective indicators, I asked leaders, "How can you tell which members are serious, and who may not be serious?" There is often a gulf between what leaders say (and believe) is their main business and their *actual* main business—as revealed by their data and their expectations of people.

So, adapting Drucker, I focused enquiries around three questions: (1) What do the leaders and people *say* (and believe) is their main business? (2) What does the data say is their *actual* main business? (3) To each of those questions, "How is business?" Typically, the church is more effective in relation to the second answer than the first; outcomes typically follow investment, time, energy, and activity. In this book, I am largely ignoring the third question in favor of the first and second. The focus is upon a congregation's main business in profession *and* performance.

The Top Ten Answers

My explorations around the first two questions have revealed a wide range of ways in which church leaders understand, or more usually assume to be, their church's main business.[1] Let's summarize the "top ten."[2]

1. For centuries, the main business of a great many churches has been *ministry to the members* and their children. Decades ago, this focused on the *pastoral care and nurture* of the members. In recent years, the paradigm extended to the *protection* of church members from the sins and secularity in the surrounding community. Sometimes, the paradigm now emphasizes the *spiritual formation* of the church's members.

2. Many churches want people to "*believe* like us." The church is rooted in a constellation of truth claims. Preaching, teaching, liturgy, and study are devoted to grounding and deepening the people in their tradition's worldview. Depending on the church, that worldview can be conservative, or liberal, or some other perspective that defies easy classification—such as Quaker, or Greek Orthodox.

3. Many churches want people to "*behave* like us." These churches have a clear moral code—prescriptions and prohibitions—to which serious people conform. The Sunday

---

1. I have published a similar, and more comprehensive, analysis of congregations (with more theological reflection) in *Church for the Unchurched*, "What People Can Become" (Nashville: Abingdon Press, 1996), 35–54.

2. In the wake of the European Enlightenment, social theorists have long presumed to define the main business of Christianity, or of "religion" in general. Durkheim explained that religion's function is to provide the shared symbols, beliefs, and values that informs a society's collective consciousness and unites the society. Marx declared that the oppressive capitalist class used religion as "the opiate of the people;" the masses, hoping for an afterlife, were anesthetized to the injustices in this life. Much more recently, in *Sacred and Secular: Religion and Politics Worldwide*, 2nd ed. (New York: Cambridge University Press, 2011) Pippa Norris and Ronald Inglehart claim that religion's main business is to provide "existential security" to a society's vulnerable people; with industrialization and development, they say, fewer people will feel vulnerable and the "demand" for religious services will decline. I have addressed their claim in *Should We Change Our Game Plan?* (Nashville: Abingdon Press, 2013), chapter 5. These three ideas are not featured in the list below, because I have not found many churches that are actually driven by any of the three ideas.

school, the children's sermon, the vacation Bible school, and other ministries present a lifestyle script for children and members.

4. Many churches, from Holiness to Pentecostal to "High Church," say that they want people to have "*experiences like ours.*" Christianity's essence is experiential; the experience can range, by tradition, from an emotional conversion, to a healing experience, to speaking in tongues, to a "sublime" experience of the Sistine Chapel or Bach's Mass in B Minor.

5. Some churches want people to "become like us," *culturally.* Their Christianity is connected to certain cultural forms, beliefs, and values, so the church wants people to speak within the tradition's vocabulary and to dress like the core members, and to share the church's values and aesthetic tastes—from food to sports to the arts to "our kind of music." (The more recent emphasis upon "diversity" and "politically correct" language in many churches would seem to nullify this paradigm. Au contraire! These churches expect new members to speak the new language and to value diversity, supremely.)

6. Some churches expect their people to "share our *politics.*" For more than a century, this agenda has expected members to be (say) Democrats or Republicans, and/or to work for causes that are achieved, at least in part, politically—from abolition or temperance historically, to abortion or several gender-related causes more recently.

7. Some churches are driven to prepare as many people as possible for *heaven.* Christianity has become mainly about going to heaven when we die. Between now and then members attend church, have a daily devotion, and live a clean life. Much of gospel music, country music, and American folk religion regard the Christian religion as a fire escape; some churches preach it.

8. Some denominations (and some of their churches) have long focused on *perpetuating* their denomination's *traditions* in such areas as creeds, liturgy, music, or polity. If the denominational tradition once crossed the Atlantic, the churches are expected to "do church" much like it was once done (say) in Germany or Scotland.

9. For some denominations, today, the priority agenda is the local church's *support for the wider institutional church.* This state of affairs represents an interesting devolution in three steps: (1) The tradition started out as a movement—reaching pre-Christian people, planting churches, and extending a Christian presence to many new places and populations. (2) In time, the movement needed an organization to support the movement; the new organization provided a hymnal, and literature, and training for pastors, and resourced the churches in many other ways. (3) Eventually, the organization became an institution; in time, it became mostly about the institution, and the churches became subservient to the institution.

10. In recent years, many churches and whole denominations have focused on *church "health"* (or "revival," or "renewal," or "vitality," or "vibrancy"). In the late twentieth century, the Natural Church Development (NCD) movement from Germany began convincing church leaders in over sixty countries that their main business was the development of "church health"—as indicated by health in eight areas of church life. NCD's influence exceeds the many churches that use their program and materials. By the fairly early twenty-first century, many denominations in many lands had bought NCD's paradigm and developed their own criteria and programs in the quest for "church health."

I have studied many churches whose leaders navigate their church's life in reference to two, three, or four of these ten themes (or

5

by some other theme). The researcher must often "dig" to discover the themes that drive a church because they are typically assumed but seldom spoken. Of course, churches (like people) may base some of their thinking, decisions, and actions upon assumptions that are not valid.

Woody Allen, decades ago, began his career in stand-up comedy. One story featured the following (alleged) experience in his life. One day, Woody felt some pain in his "chestly area." He assumed that it was heartburn, though the symptom was higher than usual. His first impulse was to see his doctor, but he guessed that he would pay twenty-five dollars for the news that he had heartburn.

Woody went to visit his buddy, whose last name was Benedict and whose nickname was "Eggs." Eggs Benedict complained of an identical discomfort in his "chestly area." Woody persuaded Eggs to go see his doctor; Eggs paid twenty-five dollars to be told that he had heartburn. Woody was silently pleased.

Two days later, Woody heard that Eggs had died. He panicked, stampeded to the local hospital, and asked for all available tests to diagnose the pain in his chestly area. Three days, many tests, and hundreds of dollars later, he learned that he had heartburn.

When Woody left the hospital, he drove over to see Eggs's mother, to express condolences. He asked, "Did Eggs suffer long?" Mrs. Benedict replied, "No. Car hit him. That was it!" (And Woody discovered he had acted on an invalid assumption.)

Spoiler Alert Number One

The driving ideas of this book can be stated in three sentences: **A church's mission, locally and globally, is its main business (or should be). The "real church" is an "ecclesia"—the "called out" people of God whom the Lord shapes into an "apostolate," then**

"sends out" to be publicly present in the world, but not of the world. This mission is a serving, witnessing, inviting outreach to all people—in their many tribes and affinity groups.

The meaning of this thesis will conclude this chapter and return in other chapters. This preview will help the following comments to make sense.

Like Woody Allen's experience, a church can act on, and even live by, a wrong assumption; more often, the assumption is secondary (or even negligible) compared to the church's main assignment from its Lord. Indeed, a church might be living by a dozen assumptions, with half of them either wrong or majoring on what the old hymn called "lesser things." Often, a church lives by several worthy values, like the ten suggested above, but is wrong in assuming that any or all of those constitute the church's *main* business. (Of course, churches have no monopoly on main-purpose confusion. Some colleges and universities, for instance, now seem more about football, or social life, or indoctrination, or preparing students for jobs than educating their students and advancing knowledge.)

Often, a church was once clear about its apostolic mission, but now, years later, it is caught in what another major management theorist, George Odiorne, once called "the activity trap." Odiorne[3] brilliantly characterized the entire life history of many types of organizations (including churches). I became aware of his insights in the years that I first perceived that many churches are beehives of programs and activities, but they do not achieve very much, and their people lack the kind of fulfillment that comes only from involvement with major achievement. (Odiorne's perspective was anticipated by advice attributed to Ernest Hemingway: "Never mistake motion for action!")

---

3. See George S. Ordione, *Management and the Activity Trap* (New York: Harper & Row, 1974).

In an earlier book, I summarize Odiorne's insights as follows. An organization

> typically begins with a clear mission and goals, and they devise programs and activities to achieve the goals and fulfill the mission. But over time, the ends are forgotten and the programs and activities become ends in themselves. The people now focus on "the way we've always done things around here." The programs and activities become impotent and less meaningful, and the organization bogs down in "the activity trap."[4]

I once heard a joke that reminded me of churches (or even whole denominations) that spin their wheels in some version of the activity trap.

A rich Arabian oil sheik had three sons. He loved his sons but had not often expressed that love. One day, he summoned his sons, told them how much he loved them, and offered to dramatize his love for them in a way they'd never forget. "Each of you, tell me your most heartfelt wish; I will grant, or exceed, your wish."

The oldest son tested the waters. "Dad, we are oil people. I want my own oil city. Give me Houston, Texas." The father replied, "I will give you the whole state of Texas."

The middle son spotted the trend. "Dad, I want my own space ship." The father replied, "I will give you all of NASA."

The youngest son had not quite caught on. "Dad, it may not sound like much, but ever since I was a little boy, I have always wanted my own Mickey Mouse outfit." The father replied, "I will give you the United Methodist Church!"

While useful as comedic hyperbole, that punch line is an over-statement. I have spent enough time in enough churches to find much to love and affirm in each one. If some of the people in a church find friendship there, or a moral compass, or glue for their

4. George G. Hunter III, *To Spread the Power: Church Growth in the Wesleyan Spirit* (Nashville: Abingdon Press, 1987), 186.

marriage, or they become rooted in prayer or scripture, or they become more compassionate, or they face death with less anxiety, or any of many other good experiences, there is enough worth in that church that the world would be better off if there were more of them. Furthermore, if a whole denomination is doing some good, we have some reason to celebrate.

And yet, a church or a denomination can be stuck in the activity trap, and profoundly underachieving, with its members (and its visitors) wondering "if this is all there is" to the Christian faith.

Emil Brunner's Way Forward

To my knowledge, there are only two ways for a church to become liberated from the activity trap and become a "real church." Both ways involve "rediscovery."

1. Some churches can rediscover, and return to, their original mission, and to the original vision, objectives, and story that once drove the church and its people to a season of achievement. Sometimes, however, the original vision was not all that clear and compelling, which may be one reason it is now eclipsed.

And often, returning to "the good old days" is no longer a live option. The community and the culture have changed, and people's language, and felt needs, and tastes in music, and attention spans, and many other things have changed. Changed to the point that, in a line attributed to Bonhoeffer, "The rusty swords of the old world are powerless to combat the evils of today and tomorrow."

2. The second, and best, way forward for most stagnant churches is to rediscover Christianity's main business, and then redefine their church's main business and become "apostolic" (or "missional") congregations.

This essentially involves two steps: (1) It involves reaching a fresh understanding of the community and the distinct populations that the church is in a position to reach, serve, and disciple. (2) It involves a serious rediscovery of the nature of the mission to which the church is called and sent.

In the early 1930s, theologian Emil Brunner reminded a Christian generation of their main business. Consider his careful, nuanced, and eloquent understanding of Christ's call—which we are meant to experience as both desire and mandate.

> The Word of God which was given in Jesus Christ is a unique historical fact, and everything Christian depends on it; hence everyone who receives this Word, and by it salvation, receives along with it the duty of passing this Word on; just as a man who might have discovered a remedy for cancer which saved himself, would be in duty bound to make this remedy accessible to all.
>
> Mission work does not arise from any arrogance in the Christian Church; mission is its cause and its life. **The Church exists by mission, just as a fire exists by burning.**
>
> Where there is no mission, there is no church; and where there is neither church nor mission, there is no faith.... Mission...is the spreading out of the fire which Christ has thrown upon the earth. He who does not propagate this fire shows that he is not burning. He who burns propagates the fire.... The divine remedy must be made accessible to all.[5]

N. T. Wright Reminds Us Why the Gospels Come First

For a generation, many church leaders quoted Brunner's lines more than any others, excepting scripture. Brunner's most famous

---

5. Emil Brunner, *The Word and the World* (London: SCM Press, 1931), 108. Emphasis and paragraphing added.

line, with one word omitted, entered the oral tradition of many Protestant Christians: "The Church exists by mission, as a fire exists by burning." By the 1980s, however, one seldom heard the line—perhaps because many of the generation's leaders no longer affirmed it, sometimes with the sidestep line, "Everything we do is mission."

Of course, when "everything" is mission, nothing is mission. Denominations cut their missionary personnel, declining morale, and membership set in at home, and the denominations have struggled to experience "renewal" (or "revitalization," or "health") ever since. Brunner's following words, while hyperbolic, became prophetic: "Where there is no mission, there is . . . no faith," and possibly "no [real] church." For decades after Brunner, theologians made many contributions, but most of the world-recognized theologians largely ignored Christianity's mission—at least in any sense the apostles would have recognized.

One significant theologian, in more recent times, now argues that many churches have failed to sufficiently understand their essential mission for at least several centuries, or longer. I am referring to N. T. Wright, and especially his book *How God Became King: The Forgotten Story of the Gospels.*[6]

Wright develops an astonishingly bold thesis. For centuries, the churches have substantially ignored the driving narrative and the pervasive meaning of all four Gospels. In this period, the church's theologians have been preoccupied with Paul's theology, or the creeds, or (more recently) with new theologies. (Indeed, Wright contends that this long-standing problem is even present in the creeds—which feature virtually nothing about Jesus between his birth and his crucifixion, as though the only chapters in Matthew's Gospel that really matter are 1, 2, 27, and 28!)

---

6. N. T. Wright, *How God Became King: The Forgotten Story of the Gospels* (New York: HarperCollins, 2012).

11

My first response was to resist Wright's challenge. After all, we all preach and teach from texts and stories from the four Gospels much of the time. And we often feature the Great Commandment and the Great Commission—from the Gospels.

True enough, so how does N. T. Wright respond to these obvious facts? He observes that we have, indeed, featured many specific texts and stories from the Gospels, but while largely ignoring the Big Story that all four of the Gospel writers were eager to tell. Wright proposes that we should sometimes read the Gospels as we do a Jane Austen novel or a Shakespeare play—not asking what a particular word, sentence, or incident means so much as asking about the overall Story the author was telling.

Furthermore, the churches have, indeed, often featured (what the Tradition calls) the Great Commandment and the Great Commission. Wright suggests, however, that the meanings of such passages are not sufficiently discovered by (say) looking up what *agape* or *ethne* meant in first-century Koine Greek. Their meaning, as in other literature, is best understood in the context of the whole Story. Wright explains that, after all, "the meaning of a word is its use in a sentence; the meaning of a sentence is its use in a paragraph; and the meaning of a paragraph is its use in the larger document to which it contributes."[7]

This grand rediscovery requires us to ask questions that were not disputed when the creeds were written, like "Why, and how, did Jesus live?" and "What did he do and teach?" and "What mandates did he give his followers?" And it involves discovering "the whole message, which is so much greater than the sum of the small parts with which we are . . . so familiar."[8] (Wright does *not* propose that we recover the Gospels and jettison the rest of the canon or the creeds; he wants to restore the Gospels to prominence within our minds.)

7. N. T. Wright, *How God Became King*, 24–25 (e-book edition).
8. Ibid., 10 (e-book edition).

The Great Love Story

I should not presume to summarize the elaborate case that N. T. Wright makes for his thesis from each of the four Gospels. No one should even attempt a *Reader's Digest* version of Wright's important book. One needs to read the book for oneself; two careful readings (especially of part 2) might be sufficient.

And space does not permit a thorough retelling of the Big Story that all four Gospels tell about Jesus, and what he and his disciples did and taught, and the mission that was entrusted to his movement for all times and places. I should, perhaps, show one man's view of the tip of the iceberg.

In the incarnation, humanity's rightful "Lord" (or "King") became one of us, Mary's son. In what he taught with authority, and in such ministries as the forgiveness of sins, the healing of diseases, the casting out of evil powers, and good news to the poor, and in ministries to lame, blind, and deaf people, to zealots, harlots, lepers, paralytics, tax collectors, and other marginal affinity groups (who were all excluded from the temple), the long-promised "kingdom" (or "reign") of Israel's High God had shifted from the distant future to the near future and, from that near future, was now edging into history and human experience.

Through his disciples, Jesus launched a New People, a New Israel, an Alternative Society that would function as a movement that would speak prophetic truth to all societies while expanding a range of outreach ministries to all sorts of people and populations, and inviting all responsive people in every "nation" to become new disciples to live no longer for themselves but for God's will, and thereby expand the movement, its ministries, and its witness.

This mission was to be Christianity's main business. Whenever, and wherever, the church is devoted to Christ's mission, it is a "real church." Real churches reject the world's way of power and pursue their ends through love, service, healing, prophesy, witness, and invitation. Jesus promised that the Holy Spirit would inspire, accompany, and empower this Messianic movement. As Wright explains: "Our 'big story' is not a power story. It isn't designed to gain money, sex, or power for ourselves.... It is a love story—God's love story, operating through Jesus and then, by the Spirit, through Jesus' followers."[9]

Spoiler Alert Number Two

There is a precondition for people to experience the Love Story and follow Christ. People need to respond to Jesus's invitation by **converting**—in the abounding sense of turning to God, opening their hearts to God's grace and will, perceiving the world through the lenses of faith, turning from their old way of life to the new, in the company of the new People of the Way. Mark tells us that Jesus launched his movement by inviting people to convert.

The Greek term *epistropho* is typically translated as "turn," "repent," or "convert." Unfortunately, the word *turn* dilutes the meaning and does not engage people today with the power that Jesus's first audiences experienced, and people now attach a moralistic meaning to the word *repent*. Terms like *convert* and *conversion*, however, point to the transformation that *epistropho* involves.

So, one indispensable goal of our outreach and mission today is (or should be) the conversion of the people whom we serve, to the end that they follow Christ, in the company of other disciples, in and beyond the church. Bishop Stephen Neill used to teach that, in New Testament conversion, a person experiences not one major turning but three—to the God who invites us in Christ, to the community of Christ, and to the kind of world that God wants. Neill's

---

9. Ibid., 241–42 (e-book edition).

model becomes enormously useful with two insights: in most converts, those turnings take place one at a time; and they happen in any conceivable sequence.[10]

Regrettably, Christianity's debunkers have convinced the secular world, and too many Christians, that inviting conversion is mere "proselytism." A six-word response to that charge comes to mind: horse feathers, fiddlesticks, tommyrot, rubbish, baloney, and balderdash. For a long time, such characters have shot at Christianity from two sides: (1) If we invite people to become Christians and join the movement, they say that we are "proselyting." (2) However, if we serve the people but do not invite them, they say that we are "paternalistic" and are perpetuating "dependency!"[11]

Fortunately, church leaders in the tradition of the apostles have no interest in letting the meaning of Christian outreach be defined by people who waste their lives assailing something they do not believe. These leaders understand that every human being has the inalienable right to experience justification and second birth, and the life of God's kingdom, and the meaning that comes from fulfilling their purpose. Those who evangelize also serve and, when we withhold that one service from people, we commit a serious sin of omission.

Our detractors still disagree. Churches, they say, should make Christian theology optional (or delete it entirely). Churches should become "inclusive," and welcome "diversity"; we should welcome

---

10. Bishop Neill tutored me in this model in a lengthy conversation in 1962. He recalled cases in which people had become the kind of Christians "who are actually useful to the kingdom" in each of the six sequences that had informed his development of the model. He added that most of Christianity's "problem" people are those who have experienced only one or two of the three turnings, and that the church must invite people to each of the three conversions. I have never found the model in Neill's published writings, but this important oral tradition obviously merits publication.

11. Over thirty years ago, Eric Berne wrote *Games Alcoholics Play*. Someday, someone will write Games Debunkers Play!

people into membership, and even leadership, whether they buy our "dogma" or not.

Actually, many churches have already tried that. I have studied such churches; they had noble motives. After all, they did not want to be "narrow-minded"; and they reasoned that in a secular society it is hard to believe anything beyond the material world and, anyway, all religions must be pretty much the same; so if people can affirm a higher reality of any sort, "you are one of us. Come on in!"

Such churches typically become the ecclesial equivalent of "mules." Mules are useful, but they are so genetically compromised that they are incapable of reproduction. Likewise, such churches are so theologically compromised that they are incapable of reproduction. Not enough new people join to replace the members they lose; they cannot retain even a bare majority of their own children into adult church membership. The more "inclusive" they become, the fewer people they include.

We can observe similar dynamics in church judicatories, institutions, and denominations. In time, at every level, the preconversion people we once welcomed want to become leaders; in more time, they change the church or institution almost beyond recognition.

Such commandeered churches, ministries, and institutions typically lose their way and their identity; often, they do not survive. One may find many cases on every continent but, in the United States, one need look no farther than many of the colleges and universities once started by churches and denominations. In what seemed like a good idea at the time, an institution welcomed professors, administrators, and trustees who did not own, or affirm, any recognizable version of the faith that started the institution. In time, the institution was "Christian" in name only; more recently, some have hidden or abandoned the name.[12]

12. The secularization of church colleges and universities is widespread and is now seldom denied. To my knowledge, James Burtchead was the first historian, in

On Overcoming an "Allergy"

For almost the first time since Emil Brunner, a globally influential theologian teams with several generations of "mission theologians," from Roland Allen to Hendrik Kraemer to David Bosch to Christopher Wright, who taught that Christianity's mission to the world is the church's main business—whose views were often dismissed with a wave of the hand because, after all, one would expect mission theologians to say such things! N. T. Wright also advances mission theology by grounding mission in the narrative common to all four Gospels.

I took some satisfaction in reading Wright's suggestion that eighteenth-century Methodism, as a sent-out movement of Christians who had experienced grace, were rooted in the Gospels, and were loving, serving, and inviting people and commending justice in the world, "might well be cited as evidence of a movement in which parts of the church did actually integrate several elements in the gospels."[13] Alas, Methodism's later history stands as proof that a movement that once got it kind of right can, over time, morph into one of the most dysfunctional institutionalized expressions of Christianity in the solar system.

I have long wondered why Protestant churches live as though they have an allergy to the Gospels. I am fairly sure of only three causes. All three causes are essentially social, in the sense that the

---

The Dying of the Light (Grand Rapids, MI: Eerdmans, 1988) to demonstrate this beyond all reasonable doubt, drawing from a range of case studies. Some Christian colleges have defied this secularizing trend by requiring that only Christians should be admitted as *students*. This, I think, has proven to be a wide (though unacknowledged) mistake for at least two reasons. First, the life of a Christian college is deepened and renewed when some students become new Christians! Second, when Christian students spend four years in a for-Christians-only educational enclave, that becomes the "new normal," and programs a generation of Christian young adults to lead churches for Christians only.

13. Wright, *How God Became King*, 36–37 (e-book edition).

people in one social group are reluctant to associate with, or be associated with, another social group: (1) The first such cause is the most obvious. To take the four Gospels seriously would prompt "respectable" Christians and churches to find ways to befriend, reach, serve, and include sidelined populations like the earliest Christian movement did. (2) In recent history, the speeches of Mother Teresa and Pope Francis have reminded us that Roman Catholics are often more rooted in the Gospels than Protestants. Anxiety about that association infects some Protestant leaders with the allergy. (3) Within Protestant Christianity, left-of-center Christians have often been more interested in the Gospels than right-of-center Christians (but less interested in the mission that gripped the Gospel writers); right-of-center Protestants, again, have often avoided the association.

So, many evangelicals seem to leave the four Gospels to the Catholics and the liberals, while the liberals (like Thomas Jefferson of old) seem to disregard the texts and passages within the Gospels that do not fit their worldview! Let me suggest that every "wing" of Protestant Christianity, and every denomination within Protestant Christianity, would experience less amnesia and more empowerment by taking the New Testament's first four books seriously. There is a reason why the four versions of the narrative were placed first in the New Testament canon. Every other book of the New Testament, like every early messianic community, regarded the narrative and teachings in those Gospels foundational. We do not need to read the New Testament epistles to figure out what the earliest Christians believed and lived for. Matthew, Mark, Luke, and John have already briefed us.

If a church or denomination became convinced that Wright is right (!), what might be the strategic response? Alas, while we hope, there is little precedent for entire institutional denominations becoming movements once again! There is, however, precedent for implementing the strategy of the "ecclesiola within the ecclesia," which refers to "parts of the church" or to movements within and from the church into the community, and to movements of people from many churches into the community, nation, and world.

Such movements require advanced commitment and competence from Christians who are called (say) to teach English as a second language, or minister with addicts, or champion the faith's expression in the arts, or plant new churches, or reach pre-Christian populations, or work against human trafficking or for creation's health.

In this paradigm, the church invites members to discover their gifts and passions, expects their committed involvement in that mission, nurtures them and prays for them, and grants serious autonomy to the ministries; the church features the ministries of the people in the church's life, newsletter, and history, and reinforces the idea in a hundred ways that merely "attending church" is not normal Christianity and following Christ in ministry *is* normal Christianity.

If the church's mission, at every level, is its main business, this nuances and expands our understanding of the role of evangelism. Traditionally, we have invited people to accept Jesus Christ "for his benefits," and of course we continue to hope that people will experience forgiveness, second birth, and new life, and face death with assurance one day.

However, the missional paradigm of the four Gospels reminds us also to hope, perhaps even more, that people will become followers of Christ in his service and movements, and thereby experience the "life that matters" that comes to people who live no longer for themselves but for God's will. Evangelism then becomes the ministry that provides new personnel for the expanding movement and its proliferating ministries. Moreover, the movement's compassionate ministries will raise Christianity's public credibility, and the movements and the churches will make more and more new disciples.

The next chapter extends such thoughts from a fresh reading of Luke's Gospel.

Chapter Two

The Earliest Outreaching Movement

The membership of "Old East Side Church" had declined for forty years. Most years, the church received a few new people—children from the confirmation class, transfers from other churches, an occasional convert. But like most churches, most years, the church lost 5–7 percent of its members as members died, or transferred to other churches, or dropped out. In a typical year, the church would receive 4–6 percent of the prior year's membership and lose 5–7 percent.

Occasional years saw exceptions. Several years, the net decline was negligible. One year, Old East Side grew 4 percent when an entourage transferred from another church in town. Two successive years reported slight growth when the pastor refused to remove any inactive names from the rolls. The succeeding pastor identified the names of members who could no longer be found, and "cleaned the rolls" (because the church was still paying "denominational taxes" on their whole listed membership!); the roster declined 12 percent that year. Most years, however, the church lost 5–7 percent of its members while receiving 4–6 percent.

Old East Side's year-by-year worship attendance reflected essentially the same gradual downward pattern; worship decline typically preceded membership decline by several years.

For most of the four decades of decline, the church's leaders were in denial. After all, they continued to receive some new people. However, when families started having fewer children and in time the confirmation classes became smaller, and a higher percentage of aging members died each year, the typical percentage of new members they received slipped more toward 3 or 4 percent than 5 or 6.

The church's leaders could financially afford denial while the declining number of members could continue to increase their contributions. Then, when three major donor families retired to the Sun Belt and two major donors died, the church experienced deficits. Staff positions were cut; programs were reduced; the church now lacked the funds and volunteers for several ministries. Someone observed, "Maybe we can't do more and more for people with fewer and fewer people to do it with." A season of soul searching (and some accusing) ensued.

"Let's Do Some Evangelism"

Then the leaders decided that the church had better "do some evangelism. We need more people." Someone recalled that the church grew in the 1950s when members walked the neighborhoods "two by two" and knocked on doors to invite people to church. So several teams tried it one evening per week for a month. Times had changed, however; gated communities and apartment communities prohibited "solicitors," and neighborhoods in which calling was still possible no longer welcomed "intrusions." The visitation did reach a family who had recently moved to town.

Someone heard that Christians could distribute tracts that presented "the way to heaven"; this project survived two weeks. A follow-up emphasis upon sharing one's testimony with people was also short lived. Old East Side scheduled a revival; church members were virtually the only attendees. Someone (kind of) quoted Jesus as telling his followers to simply "let your light shine before men." Someone else replied, "That is what we have been doing for forty years!"

Someone said, "Maybe we ought to invite unchurched people for their sake, rather than to prop up our church." While the leaders nodded in agreement, beyond that they were stymied. They turned to their shared knowledge of the Bible. They'd always aspired to be a biblical church, and they agreed that they had tried to do evangelism in the ways they assumed the Bible prescribes—like the visiting, witnessing, testifying, and revivals.

Precedents for Turning to the Bible

This chapter essentially agrees with Old East Side's leaders that the biblical revelation can teach us ways to reach pre-Christian people. Like many church leader groups, however, the leaders read the Bible devotionally, but they neglected to read it to inform their theology, or ministry, or outreach, or much else in church life, because they assume that they already knew what it teaches! (Somewhat like the hero in the film *American Sniper*, who carries his Bible but never reads it because he already knows what is in it: "God, country, family!")

This chapter's burden is to demonstrate that the New Testament reveals perspectives on the ministry of evangelism that, for a long time, have escaped the attention of most church leaders. It would not be appropriate to expect some text or passage to give a prescription for reaching (say) a middle-aged, bisexual, disillusioned-with-Marxism Eskimo! Since perhaps no two people become Christians in exactly the same way, effective evangelism is specific to the context, the people, their issues, and the Holy Spirit's lead. But the New Testament gives the indispensable foundation for approaching pre-Christian populations in the tradition of the apostles and their movements.

This is not, of course, a new idea—as two well-known examples will remind us.

For at least a century, witnessing Christians drew from verses in Paul's letter to the Romans and presented "The Roman Road" to people. While the expression of five affirmations has varied some, this is typical:

1. All have sinned, and have fallen short of the glory of God. (3:23)

2. The "wages" (or consequence) of our sin is "death." (6:23)

3. God loves us, and Christ died for us, to give us eternal life. (6:23, 5:8)

4. If we believe God raised Jesus from death, and we confess him, we will be saved. (10:9-10)

5. We are now justified by grace and have peace with God. (5:1)

Again, for at least a half century, Latin American Protestants in the "New Life for All" movement have often drawn from verses and themes in John's Gospel to share a similarly scripted set of affirmations that also vary some in expression. The approach is especially rooted in John 10:10 ("I am come that they might have life, and that they might have it more abundantly" [KJV]), but usually without specific scripture references attached to each statement:

- God created all people for Life.

- In their Sin, people have lost the Life they were meant for.

- God came in Jesus Christ to offer New Life to all people.

- People can receive this New Life by turning—from their sins, and to Christ in trust and obedience, and to the Community of New Life.

- We are called to be faithful to that New Life in all of our relationships.

Both scripts have enjoyed a significant history. Church leaders once invented them "on the fly," and they "stuck" in people's minds and informed many ministries of witness. I have, in my own ministry, sometimes said these things to people, and grace visited the conversation, and people responded.

There is no reason, however, to avoid reflecting on them. As a theologian, I have come to especially appreciate the New Life for All approach, because it does not begin with the fall; it begins (where the Bible does) with creation, and its fifth point alludes to the kingdom ethic that Christians are called to live by. Usually, pre-Christian people do not already know that they are created in God's image, for a significant life and purpose; and, lest they mistake Christianity as merely a free pass to happiness now and heaven later, they need to know something about the new way of life to which Christ calls his disciples.

There is no reason, of course, to assume that Romans and John have now been so thoroughly mined for their gold that Christian leaders have no need to revisit those books! Furthermore, there are reasons to not rely excessively on memorized scripts to communicate the good news. The people in many Christian movements preach, teach, and tell stories, and use analogy, music, art, drama, literature, film, liturgy, and other expressions to communicate truth and hope; and, in every generation and culture, the Ministry of Conversation is imperative.

Returning to the New Testament, Again

As I read N. T. Wright's challenge to take the four Gospels seriously, I recalled that, in the very early Christian movement's history—as reflected in the four Gospel narratives, Jesus and his disciples expanded the new movement *as* they engaged in a kind of "evangelism," which continued in the period reported in the Acts of the Apostles. Christianity's earliest leaders invited people to become followers of Jesus who would learn from him, and become committed to his way, and love and serve people, and tell the good news, and invite more and more people to follow this way. I propose that if twenty-first-century churches, in the West and elsewhere, learned how the very earliest evangelizers approached outreach, they'd find ways to become apostolic movements once again.

I have suggested that rooting our approach to evangelism in the Bible is not a new idea. Indeed, most of the churches that do evangelism within their culture, and mission across cultures, cite scriptural precedents for their approach. I have, however, often been amazed at the extent to which texts can serve as pretexts; leaders may even attach their own meanings to scripture. Once "we" define ourselves as "a biblical church," a leader group may come to assume that whatever "we" do is "biblical."

This is not my first published reflection from scripture to understand how we help people become new Christians. I devote chapters in several books to such study. Perhaps most notably, the first chapter of *Radical Outreach* demonstrates that Paul's two letters to the church at Corinth can be read as "a Great Commission Manual."[1]

Three Surprises from the Gospel of Luke

More recently, standing on N. T. Wright's shoulders, I have wondered what we might discover about Christianity's outreach if we rediscovered the very earliest movement's approaches as reflected in the Gospels. Let me feature this possibility by drawing from a fresh study of the Gospel of Luke (which is often, if not usually, the best Gospel for a seeker to begin with).[2] From the vantage point of the many churches like Old East Side, let's begin with some initial observations.

First, nowhere in the Gospel of Luke are people invited to accept Jesus Christ so they can go to heaven. People were invited to become "disciples" (followers of Christ who would band together to learn his gospel and ethic and live by the will and power of God) and love, serve, and invite people. Luke's Gospel does not ignore, but

---

1. For instance, Paul makes clear (1 Cor 4) that we cannot totally rely on the movement's few full-time people, such as the apostles, to spread the gospel; the mission is entrusted to all disciples. Our role as disciples in the world (2 Cor 5) is analogous to the role of an ambassador. In that role we are not mere "peddlers" for Christianity; we are "agents" of reconciliation. Paul makes clear that making new Christians does not typically happen instantly, but is often a process over time: "I planted, Apollos watered, but God made it grow" (1 Cor 3:6). Paul teaches (2 Cor 10) that local movements are called to also be involved in the much wider mission. In these points, and others, Paul becomes astonishing specific in ways that could form church leaders today. For a fuller Corinthian perspective, see my *Radical Outreach: The Recovery of Apostolic Ministry and Evangelism* (Nashville: Abingdon Press, 2003), 22–40.

2. I have observed that some churches feature Mark's Gospel when they are engaging people with addiction and other "power" issues. When churches are engaging Jewish or other Semitic people, they often feature Matthew's Gospel. When churches engage philosophically inclined people, they may feature John's Gospel. In a majority of cases, however, churches in outreach initially feature Luke's Gospel, and they may begin with Luke 15.

27

rather assures, our life after death. Zechariah's vision within the birth narrative involves "light to those who are sitting...in the shadow of death" (Luke 1:79). In Luke 10, when the Seventy-Two return from their mission, Jesus invites them to "rejoice...that your names are written in heaven" (v. 20). But nowhere in Luke is heaven offered as an incentive to believe in, or follow, Jesus.

Consistent with this, the early disciples did not seem to try to "sell" people on following Jesus for any other "benefits." His benefits, like healing and exorcism, were apparently extended to people in need whether they ever became disciples or not; some did, some did not. There were cases in which a person's faith, or a parent's faith, facilitated a healing or deliverance; in most cases, we are not told whether they ever followed him in the movement.

Second, the early disciples never invited people to "attend our church." They invited people to follow Jesus in his emergent movement that, for those who followed, was a different experience than the later experience of attending an institutional parish church. Nowhere in Luke's Gospel is being a follower of Christ about "attending church." Did they meet in some social structure for worship, teaching, and fellowship? Yes, but like football players who attend team meetings, the game wasn't mainly about attendance.[3]

In the first-century Mediterranean world, many people gathered in, and contributed to their community through, "voluntary associations" such as extended "households" and "congregations."[4]

---

3. If you are interested in the relevance of sports metaphors to understanding our challenge today, see George G. Hunter III, *Should We Change Our Game Plan?* (Nashville: Abingdon Press, 2013).

4. See Michael S. Moore, "Civic and Voluntary Associations in the Greco-Roman World," in Joel B. Green and Lee Martin McDonald, *The World of the New Testament: Cultural, Social, and Historical Contexts* (Grand Rapids: Baker Publishing Group, 2013), chapter 11. Drawing from the earlier work of Wayne Meeks and others, Moore features four types of organized life in the culture of that period: the household, the voluntary association (some writers use the term congregation), the philosophical school, and the synagogue.

As a culturally indigenous movement, earliest Christianity undoubtedly gathered into similar groups.[5] In time, those groups apparently morphed into the house churches and the somewhat larger de facto congregations reflected in Acts and later writings.

Since Christian faith is even "more caught than taught," seekers were undoubtedly welcomed, even invited, into the fellowship and experiences of these voluntary associations. It could even happen spontaneously. An extended "household" typically met at someone's home, often outside in the courtyard. A larger congregation typically met in a very public setting. Passersby could drop in! I have observed a similar dynamic in sub-Sahara Africa, where many congregations gather in, or adjacent to, public space. It may be in the open air; there may be a roof, but with open sides. Everyone who walks by and appears at all interested is invited to join the celebration.

Third, in stark contrast to the meetings and activities of the many reclusive, even secretive, religious associations of the ancient Mediterranean world, virtually everything in the very early Jesus movement happened publicly, in the open, where the town's people walked, traded, and conversed. (Even the apparent exceptions illustrate my point. Jesus sometimes taught in a synagogue or even in the temple; his ministry of conversation sometimes took place in someone's home. But all of this was not on the Jesus movement's turf; they had no turf, and apparently little need of it.) Jesus and his band (in

---

5. Moore mentions that "philosophical schools" were another type of organization in this period; I have never found evidence that the very early Christian movement founded anything like these. The fourth type of social organization one found most everywhere was the Jewish synagogue. But because Jesus's movement reached all sorts of people, including lepers, paralytics, blind and deaf people, and many others who were excluded from the Temple and synagogue, his movement apparently did not replicate any Jewish social order—such as the exclusive fellowships of the Pharisees, or the closed community of the Qumran people, or the rabbinic academies. (See Daniel J. Harrington, "Church, Life and Organization of," in *The New Interpreter's Dictionary of the Bible*, Volume 1 [Nashville: Abingdon Press, 2006], 658.)

time, it swelled to an entourage) walked from town to town, village to village. Most of the ministry was in a very public setting. Much of Jesus's teaching was in a public setting. And Jesus was observed, in open public places, to befriend and fraternize with "tax collectors and sinners."

In a word, each local movement began as Jesus's people practiced radical "presence." They were in, but not of, the world. They were the in-breaking reign's "salt" and "light" in each community.

Today, the lack of a "critical mass" of Christians who are visibly present in their communities may be the biggest single barrier to churches becoming local movements. With the secularization of the West, a great many churches have circled the wagons, often withdrawing into Christian enclaves or networks in which Christians socialize with each other; buy their homes, furniture, appliances, and cars from Christians; exercise at the church's gym (rather than the local health club); homeschool their kids or send them to private school (rather than the public school); and send their kids to Christian colleges (rather than state or secular colleges), while preparing to eventually retire in a residential facility for senior Christians. As Pope Francis has observed, far too many Christians now live in "a ghetto of our own making."[6]

The tradeoffs from this silent shift are subtle, but cumulative and enormous. With fewer Christian kids in the public schools and fewer Christian parents in the PTA, with fewer Christians fraternizing with fellow sufferers at Gold's Gym, with fewer Christians befriending and interacting with pre-Christian people almost everywhere in the community, the churches unwittingly contribute to the further secularization of their community, and the relational chasm between the church and the community expands.

---

6. Francis X. Rocca, "Pope Francis and the New Rome," *Wall Street Journal,* April 3, 2015, http://www.wsj.com/articles/pope-francis-and-the-new-rome-1428075101.

In many communities today, the pre-Christian populations have heard so many bad things about churches and they rub shoulders with so few serious Christians, they no longer perceive that becoming Christians is a plausible thing for people like them to consider. In his book *The Sacred Canopy*, Peter Berger shows us that "secularization has resulted in a widespread collapse of the plausibility of traditional definitions of reality." Into the void marched "pluralism," many alternative worldviews now "compete" with Christianity for people's attention and allegiance.[7] Since Berger wrote, more and more churches have withdrawn from the competition; the Christian retreat from the marketplace of ideas has abandoned millions of lost people to a pantheon of idols. Decades ago, church leaders and their people reduced the Great Commission to the Great Omission; we now observe the Great Abdication.

More recently, other writers have sounded this alarm. Christianity needs, once again, to be in the world, while not of it. Perhaps the most important voice is another sociologist. In James Davison Hunter's *To Change the World*, the third essay is devoted to "A Theology of Faithful Presence."[8] Hunter observes three characteristic Christian approaches to engaging secular modernity in recent history: some churches want to remain "pure" in the face of modernity, some want to "defend" the faith from the challenges of modernity, and some want to be "relevant" to this emerging world (by "letting the world write the agenda!").

Hunter calls the churches to an alternative way that begins with making disciples who become more like Jesus the Christ, who enter the world, and live primarily in the world, as agents of God's

---

7. See Peter L. Berger, *The Sacred Canopy: Elements of a Sociological Theory of Religion* (New York: Integrated Media, 1966), especially chapter 6.

8. See *To Change the World: The Irony, Tragedy, and Possibility in the Late Modern World* (New York: Oxford University Press, 2010). I have reordered Hunter's three observations, and some of the interpretations are my own.

shalom—engaging the world's people and places in love, service, challenge, and invitation.

So, in the earliest movement, it was mainly about following Christ with his people in the community; it was not mainly about going to church now and going to heaven later.

Perspectives on Outreach from the Gospel of Luke

In Luke's account, Jesus and the first generation of disciples were primarily with the people, in their communities, as salt and light. The recovery of a Christian presence and public ministry in a fallen world, whose lost people may fall for almost anything, may be the most important strategic insight for twenty-first-century Christians to take away from a reading of Luke's Gospel. Several other themes show what Christian movements might have in mind, and do, next.

First, in Luke 1, the Magnificat reminds us that the life of the kingdom of God is not merely for the soul, the family, and the afterlife. The Christian's vision of a world in which God's will is done on earth, as in heaven, plants the seeds of moral, social, and economic reform. In Luke 11, Jesus critiques the Pharisees for obeying the mere rules of their tradition while "neglecting justice and love for God" (v. 42). One may infer, from the broad "pro-life" revelation in Luke 12, that the sparrows, ravens, and lilies matter to God, that creation care is a mandate.[9]

Second, in chapters 2–5 and elsewhere, Luke makes clear that the God of Abraham has sent the Savior for the sake of all people, peoples, and affinity groups—conspicuously including tax collectors,

---

9. We learned in the Christian world mission, long ago, that foreign missionaries cannot be the public leaders in the quest for reform in the host society, lest they be sent home! God entrusts the work and advocacy for social reform to the indigenous church.

zealots, lepers, people who were paralyzed or crippled or mute or sick or lame or blind or deaf or insane or possessed, as well as infants, children, women, slaves and masters, prostitutes, Samaritans, Gentiles and other people—most of whom were excluded from Israel's temple.

The earliest ministry was, by no means, confined to such marginalized affinity groups. The outreach included vocational groups from fishermen to lawyers to at least one centurion and one "rich young ruler," and to Pharisees, Sadducees, and other Jews, and to other "regular" people. Luke 7–8 reports ministry to a widow and her dead son, and to a woman who "is a sinner" (7:39) and to a synagogue leader and his daughter.

However, the scandal and notoriety that his enemies attached to Jesus came from his movement's love and hope for people excluded from the temple and for other unwanted people. They repeatedly charged that Jesus was "a friend of...sinners" (7:34). (Today, churches sometimes adapt the principle of reaching sidelined populations by simply engaging and inviting all the people they can find that no other church seems to be interested in!)

Third, in chapter 5, Jesus invited some fishermen to join him in the movement and become "fishers of men" (see v. 10). Their good news featured the forgiveness of sins as well as the power of God's reign in healing and deliverance; later in Luke's Gospel, Jesus dramatizes the message of justification by grace through faith.[10] When people respond to the invitation to receive forgiveness and follow Christ, joining the movement involves repentance, faith, and baptism. Luke, with the other Gospel writers, makes clear that disciples are called to "fish" for people who are "lost," like sheep without a shepherd, who

---

10.   See the parable of the Pharisee and the tax collector in Luke 18:9-14. Also run (do not walk) to read the exposition of this passage in chapter three of Joachim Jeremias, *The Central Message of the New Testament* (Minneapolis: Fortress Press, 1981).

need to be found and cannot find by themselves the life they were born for and yearn for. Disciples are mandated to "bear fruit." The Lord's "harvest" exceeds the number of people available to gather it.

Individuals who had experienced grace were urged to share their good news. In Luke 8, a man delivered from possession was directed to "return home, and tell the story of what God has done for you" (v. 39).

Nevertheless, the movement typically did outreach ministry in teams. This is clear in Luke 9 where Jesus sends out the Twelve and in Luke 10 where he sends out the Seventy-two—two by two, and later in the apostolic bands reported in Luke's Acts of the Apostles. (The Seventy-two were sent out primarily to prepare villages for Jesus's scheduled visit.)

The parable of the sower in Luke 8 features the priority of planting the "seed" of God's Word on "good soil." This means, in part, to find and reach people who are receptive to God's leading and empowering presence, which would be consistent with the suggestion in Luke 9 that disciples should not squander time with people who do not, for now, welcome the messengers and the message.

Fourth, "the Sermon on the Plain" in Luke 6 features Jesus teaching a new way of life—featuring themes such as the Golden Rule, good deeds, mercy, nonjudgmental love, forgiveness, and even good will toward enemies—publicly and early in the movement's mission. In Luke 12, Jesus declares that his way is incompatible with materialism. He explains that the way of the reign of God involves living a new life, living by the will of God, in the company of the new people of God. (Similar teachings are prominent in the Matthew 5–7 "Sermon on the Mount," which was also presented early and publicly.)

It is important to see this ethic as prominent within Jesus's **public** teaching, because a significant book once planted some enduring seeds of confusion. In 1936, C. H. Dodd published *The Apostolic*

Preaching and Its Development.[11] The book was a monumental achievement. Generations of Christian leaders have been indebted to Dodd. He inferred, from sources like the outline of the Gospel of Mark and the evangelistic speeches in the Acts of the Apostles, the essential content of the kerygma (the message that the apostles and all of Christ's other ambassadors had in common).

C. H. Dodd gave us two enormously important insights for publicly presenting the faith today: (1) Only somewhat like the Roman Road, the Four Spiritual Laws, New Life for All, and the other scripts that were so popular in the twentieth century, the apostles and their people had the same essential message in mind, although that kerygma had multiple themes[12] and was more profound and transformative than the more recent projects. (2) Apparently, however, the apostles never simply recited a memorized speech; from a general script, they spoke extemporaneously and imaginatively to a wide range of audiences. As Jesus apparently ministered to each person at least somewhat differently, the apostles apparently never delivered exactly the same speech to any two audiences. (Furthermore, they were even more concerned to communicate the message's meaning than its content.)

In addition to the kerygma, Dodd also featured the Didache—the early movement's compendium of ethical teaching. The Didache was lost for many centuries, but a Greek manuscript was discovered in the nineteenth century; Dodd brought it to increased attention.

---

11. C. H. Dodd, *The Apostolic Preaching and It's Development: Three Lectures, with an Appendix on Eschatology and History* (New York: Harper and Brothers, 1936).

12. The New Testament's writers tell us about the gospel of the kingdom of God, the righteousness of God, the grace of God, and the love of God; and about the good news of forgiveness, adoption, reconciliation, redemption, justification, second birth, sanctification, healing, deliverance, peace, and the restored image of God within us; and a new covenant, a new Israel, a new humanity, and a new heaven and earth, abundant life and eternal life, and much more in what Paul called (in Eph 3:8) "the immeasurable riches of Christ."

For some reason, however, Dodd claimed that the material of the Didache was not intended for public knowledge, but was reserved for converts and other Christians.

That conclusion is dubious, for at least three reasons: (1) Much of the material in the Didache is from Jesus's teaching in Luke 6 and Matthew 5–7. Both Luke and Matthew are clear that Jesus taught these ideas publicly, with no suggestion that they were private, for disciples only. (2) The first line of the Didache tells us what it was and who it was for: "Teaching of the Lord to the Nations by the Twelve Apostles." (3) One of the perennial questions that lost seekers ask, in every generation and perhaps in every culture, is the question of how to live their life, and what to live it for. Seekers are often more interested in that question than any other. There are no good reasons to withhold the knowledge of that way until after people believe.

Fifth, and finally, Luke 15 presents a towering set of insights for local Christian movements today. We are all familiar with the three parables of the lost coin, the lost sheep, and the lost son. Some of us are familiar with the fact that the three parables are redundant; they all make the same points: (1) Something of great value is lost. (2) In response, there is a search or a vigil. (3) When the lost coin, sheep, or son is found, there is rejoicing and celebration.

We may also know that the rhetorical agenda of the three stories is that the audience, upon hearing them and reflecting upon them, may make the Great Discovery that Israel's God, now present and revealed in Jesus of Nazareth, is the Searcher—analogous to the woman, the shepherd, and the father.

The narratives, and Luke's Grand Narrative, remind us that to communicate the good news, the early Christian movement did not rely primarily on the truth being mediated through propositional statements; the movement engaged people's imaginations. Each of the four Gospels is a version of the Grand Story that can catalyze the discovery(s) that can lead to reconciliation and the new life. Each

Gospel features many specific narratives within the grand narrative. In time the movement expanded its repertoire to music, drama, the visual arts, and many other genres of expression, in addition to conversation, teaching, preaching, and telling the stories and the Story.

We have *not* mined all the gold in Luke's Gospel; indeed, his strategic insights continue in his second volume—the Acts of the Apostles. I have not stressed that this early movement was a **lay** movement; no one in this early history was "ordained" in the sense that any Christian tradition now means it.[13] We have not featured the most indispensable single principle in the ministry of evangelism— the "Ministry of Conversation," which is reflected most prominently in the Gospel of John. We have mentioned the wide practice of encouraging seekers to begin with a reading of Luke's Gospel. Churches that engage addictive populations, or populations with obsession, control, or power issues often encourage people to begin with the Gospel of Mark. Moreover, the five teaching sections of the Gospel of Matthew served as an early catechism: many churches today have found Matthew to be an indispensable study for new disciples.

A Contemporary Case Study

We close this chapter with one inescapable question. Times have changed in two thousand years, and every church in every place is now called to serve and reach people in a culture that is different from the first-century, Aramaic-speaking, Galilean-cultural setting for most of Luke's narrative. What might the adaptation and application of some of these themes look like in ministry today? While

13. In the second and third chapters of *Should We Change Our Game Plan?* (Nashville: Abingdon Press, 2013) I developed the themes that earliest Christianity was a lay movement that typically did outreach ministry in teams, and what this looks like today.

no specific model is likely to fit everywhere, the following case study dramatizes the possibility everywhere.

Victory Christian Fellowship (recently renamed "Victory"), in the Philippines, was birthed in Manila in 1984. A team of sixty-five students and missionaries from the United States spent the summer in Manila, in outreach to college students. Team members spoke in the open air and in settings where students naturally gathered, they engaged in thousands of conversations, they engaged in ministries as needed, they led groups for seekers, and they invited receptive students to evangelistic celebrations that met each evening at a Girl Scouts auditorium. By summer's end, a congregation of 150 members had formed, meeting in a cinema.

Three decades later, Victory is an urban Philippine Christian movement with more than 120,000 members. The church celebrates and serves at fifteen different locations in metropolitan Manila, and in seventy-seven "provincial churches" in urban centers across the Philippines. Each location (or "campus") schedules multiple congregations every weekend.

Victory is a lay-driven, evangelical, charismatic Christian movement. The movement is not "personality centered"; no Victory pastor is regarded as a "celebrity." Victory's mission is, simply stated, "Honor God. Make Disciples." They interpret the statement to mean that their central goal for people is not so much to get people converted, saved, or ready for heaven as to help them become "real followers" of Jesus Christ.

Victory emphasizes three essential features of discipleship: (1) Disciples **follow** Jesus Christ as Lord, living by his word and will. (2) Disciples meet in **fellowship** (in weekly "Victory Groups") with one another, in study, prayer, support, and encouragement. (3) Disciples **fish** for lost people who need to be found, through friendships, ministry, witness, and invitation. (The features are often blended; seekers are included in the life of Victory Groups before they experience faith.) I have stressed those three features somewhat in ascending order because, within Victory's many ministries, their **main business** is to reach, invite, and form new disciples.

Since every Victory Group needs a leader, the movement has developed training courses for small group leaders and other courses for other people engaged in a range of ministries, including church planters and missionaries. Victory has sent missionaries (some short-term, some long-term) to peoples of seventeen nations—mainly across much of Asia. (Ninety percent of the movement's long-term missionaries first served as short-term missionaries.) In the Philippines, where most of the ministry is entrusted to gifted, trained, and supported laity, Victory has experienced almost 25 percent net growth for each of the last twelve years.

The Victory movement acknowledges its limitations. It cannot lead congregations in all of the many languages spoken in the Philippines' several thousand islands, nor can it serve and reach across the nation's vast demographic range. (For instance, Victory is not prepared to engage tribal peoples or nonliterate populations.) In many locations, Victory provides medical, dental, food, and other ministries, but there are some ministries it cannot take on; it refers people to churches with those ministries, and may support those ministries financially. Victory specializes in ministry with college students, and its Real Life Foundation provides scholarships for increasing numbers of students who otherwise could not experience a higher education.

This growing Christian movement faces serious ongoing challenges. The most serious challenge is identifying and training enough Victory Group leaders. Although Victory's model calls for every disciple to be meeting in a small group, only half of the members are involved in a group. Nevertheless, in Metro Manila alone, Victory has people meeting weekly in over 7,100 groups.

Victory faces another challenge in moving its laity from mere church attendees to volunteers in ministry. In a study of five of the

Manila churches, three were deploying up to a quarter of their attendees in ministry; the other two involved about 12 percent of attendees in ministry. (Since not all attendees are members, the percentage of members in volunteer ministry is higher.) The leaders are aware that too many people are "slashers"—people who serve in more than one ministry role.

Victory deploys theologically educated people to serve as pastors, church planters, missionaries, and campus leaders and also trains additional leaders for such roles within the movement. The church's leaders learn from each other about the trends and needs in their target population that they are observing and the best practices in ministry that they are discovering.

Victory Metro East, where Winston Reyes is the lead pastor, is one of the fifteen Victory locations in Metro Manila. This campus of Victory Christian Fellowship launched in 2009, in a cinema theater in a shopping mall in Pasig City. Within a month, they had expanded to four congregations.

Today, one will find most of Victory Metro East's congregations at a rented space that seats eight hundred on the mall's fourth level. That space hosts two youth services on Friday evenings and six congregations on Sundays (at 9:00 and 11:00 a.m., and 1:00, 3:00, 5:00, and 7:00 p.m.). Another four congregations still meet in a theater on Sunday afternoon and evening. The children and youth ministries, as well as the church offices and other activities, also occupy rented space in the mall. Total attendance per weekend now exceeds 7,500.

Victory Metro East has nine pastors, several administrative staff, and other personnel deployed in ministry to the six major schools in their ministry area, but most of the ministry is done by laity—including 575 group leaders, whose groups dot the public landscape—meeting in coffee houses, restaurants, offices, and campuses, as well as public settings in the mall. Victory Metro East is rapidly outgrowing the available space in the mall. They plan to plant another Victory constellation of congregations in another mall in the nearby city of Antipolo.

By now, I have more than hinted of the supreme way that the Victory movement reflects the third point of this chapter. Somewhat like the earliest Jesus movement in Galilee, Victory is an intentionally **public** Christian movement; the church practices radical **presence**. They especially love to plant churches in malls; the reason becomes obvious when once stated. The Philippine Islands have such a hot, humid, tropical climate that virtually no one fully acclimates to the climate. Shopping malls are now omnipresent in the cities and in many large towns. Shopping malls are air-conditioned. Enormous numbers of people go to the malls on weekends and whenever they can, to browse, shop, meet friends, watch a movie, or hang out—and cool off! As Winston Reyes explains, "The malls have become the center of city life in our country."

So the Victory movement plants new churches in malls whenever possible. Occasionally, Victory churches occupy auditoriums, theaters, or renovated warehouses. Pastor Reyes explained that a setting must meet several criteria. It needs to be publicly visible and accessible, in a strategic location, and near campuses. In every location, a new church (and most of its groups and ministries) needs to occupy public space, or space that is adjacent to and open to public space, where people gather or walk by. Greeters are positioned to invite anyone who appears interested to "Come on in!"

Chapter Three

Sojourning with the Muscle Crowd

Compared to anything that most of our forbears in the faith experienced, or could have imagined, the world that God calls the churches to engage, serve, and love is changing—more rapidly, and more unpredictably, than ever before. So far, the twenty-first century has been the Age of Surprises. The one thing that we now know for sure about the future is that it will surprise us!

The Church's Shifting Place in a Secular Era

The most significant and pervasive of the changes, however, is no recent visitor. The secularization of the West, which has sidelined and shriveled Christianity's influence in Western culture, began with the Renaissance and the Enlightenment; then forces like science, industrialization, urbanization, globalization, competing ideologies, and chic skepticism have intensified the rate of secularization.[1] Among

---

1. While avoiding too much technical history, I have explained the character and significance of such secularizing events in *How to Reach Secular People* (Nashville: Abingdon, 1992) and, more recently, in *Should We Change Our Game Plan?* (Nashville: Abingdon, 2012). Those books also report what some Christian

the educated classes, "philosophical materialism"[2] has become the dominant worldview, while the less educated classes have typically reverted, at the level of meaning, to folk religion and folk wisdom (often with a Christian veneer).

In this changing environment, the church has lost the "home field advantage" it enjoyed for a thousand years. In response, many churches have "circled the wagons." Their driving agenda is protecting their people from the world rather than being "in but not of" the world, as "salt" and "light."

This means that "job one" for many churches is to love the city again, with all the opportunities that open up, with any risks that are involved.[3] After all, Christianity's "presence" in the community is a prerequisite to doing anything else for the community and its people. Disengaged long-distance outreaches toward the world, from bumper-sticker slogans to denominational convention resolutions, are nice tries only.

The Great Suggestion: Christian Presence in Human Communities

When, in field seminars with church leaders, I have advocated the recovery of a robust Christian presence in communities everywhere,

---

advocates and churches are doing to engage the secular people that secularization has shaped.

2. The clearest explanation of what most educated secular people now seem to believe (or assume) that I have found is Rupert Sheldrake's *Science Set Free: 10 Paths to New Discovery* (New York: Random House, 2012). Sheldrake summarizes the same ten points in a famous TED Talk that is available on the Internet: www .youtube.com/watch?v=JKHUaNAxsTg.

3. Often, Christian leaders vastly exaggerate the risks involved in following Christ in the world. Missional church leaders, however, select and prepare their people for penetrating some community sector or affinity group, they go forth in teams, they pray before and debrief after each excursion. See chapters 2 and 3 of *Should We Change Our Plan?* (Nashville: Abingdon, 2013) for a fuller discussion of outreach ministry by laity, in teams.

their eyes typically glaze over. If I can even prompt a conversation, someone inevitably asks what our presence in the world would even look like, or feel like.[4]

I usually respond to the question autobiographically. I reflect from six decades of experiences with the "muscle crowd," and my more recent six-year experience with people in the genre of magic known as "mentalism." Several years ago, a chance conversation on an airplane reminded me of my role, and what I have been doing, in my involvement with the affinity groups who "pump iron" and "read minds."

On a flight to London, the fellow sitting next to me was an obvious professor-type. (I told you I became a mind reader!) When I asked about his vocation, I learned he was indeed a university professor! (In mentalism, we call that a "hit"!) I asked, "What do you teach?" He replied, "Politics." I asked him, "Do you mean 'political science'?" He slammed his fist on his seat tray and virtually shouted, "It is *not* a science!" (I had stumbled into a conversation with a history!)

When he came back down, he explained. When his academic field was young, the sciences dominated the American academy, politically. The leaders of any younger academic field were pressured to call their field a "science"—*if* they wanted a place in the university, with recognition, funding, and so on. The professor reported that his department was one of the first to "come out of the closet" and go public with the fact that, while the field engages in the serious study of political history, philosophy, systems, practices and so on, it is not accurate to say that it is a "science."

Further in the conversation, I learned that my new friend was en route to Moscow. His specialty is Russian politics, specifically the interface of the Russian people with their government. Avocationally, my new friend plays in jazz bands. Every seventh (sabbatical) semester, he plays his sax in a Moscow jazz band. As he converses

---

4. When we have circled the wagons long enough, amnesia has set in!

with musicians and fans, and as he overhears people's daytime conversations in many settings, he learns what the Russian people think about their issues, their government, and their nation's life. He summarized his role, "Like a cultural anthropologist, I am a participant observer."

In seminars I tell that story and then share some of what I have learned about trends and patterns in a secular society from my participant observations with the exercise crowd and with performers who entertain audiences by demonstrating ESP. I always comment that I find contact and fellowship in these sectors more interesting, *and* I become a better theologian, than I would experience in spending *all* of my time with the saints and always secluded within my comfort zone. While I could write a book from these experiences, this chapter and the next will show the tips of the two icebergs.

My Decades with the Muscle Crowd

My involvement with the fitness subculture began in the 1950s. At fourteen, raised in Miami, Florida, I was the skinny kid who got sand kicked in his face at the beach. I acquired a barbell and a bench, turned part of our garage into a home gym, put exercise posters on the wall, and read most of the monthly articles in *Strength and Health* and *Iron Man*. (Several times I succumbed to the ads that promised "barn door lats" or a "six-pack in thirty days" before I became a *discriminating* reader of ads!) In two years, I gained forty pounds of muscle and became a student leader and a power hitter on my high school baseball team.

For my sixteenth birthday, my dad gave me my first summer membership at the York Athletic Club—then managed by Stan Stanczyk, an Olympic weightlifting champion. Mr. Stanczyk was a serious Polish Catholic Christian, but at least half of the York guys were "secular." They'd never been influenced by any viable version of the Christian faith. Most of them were not atheists, or agnostics, but "ignostics"—they had no idea what Christians were even talking about. As I overheard hundreds of conversations, and sometimes participated, I learned a lot about their beliefs, values, questions, issues, agendas, illusions, and idols. (No one was yet saying, "I am spiritual but not religious," and the term *pumping iron* had not yet been invented.)

I lifted weights throughout college and divinity school, in the weight room in the school gymnasiums. I entered some weightlifting contests and took home an occasional medal. Then in 1962, while still in divinity school, I had a saturation experience in secularity; I spent the summer in ministry with the daytime inhabitants of "Muscle Beach" in Southern California. Most of the people who befriended me that summer were very secular—indicated by negligible familiarity with the Ten Commandments and even less familiarity with the Lord's Prayer. They had no idea what I was talking about, no recognition of Christianity's most treasured language and symbols, no church to one day "return" to; many could not even tell me the name of the church that their parents or grandparents stayed away from!

While most of my Muscle Beach friends had those features in common, that seemed to be about all. They were a population mosaic. So I was in friendship and ministry with bodybuilders and beatniks, gays and lesbians, surfers and sunbathers, alcoholics and "druggies," shopkeepers and "beach bums," and others. Each group had some shared interests, attitudes, beliefs, and values, as well as even shared jargon and aesthetic tastes, that made them different from the other subcultures, making each group quite homogeneous. There was little communication between one group and another; power lifters didn't fraternize with beatniks.

Fortunately, there were clear locations where I could go to engage people in almost any piece of the mosaic. So I worked out and conversed with the muscle crowd at Muscle Beach's open-air "weight pen."[5] I conversed with gay people at a canopied open-air tavern. I conversed, and more openly advocated the Christian faith, in the evenings at a beatnik coffee shop; every evening featured an open microphone and fairly civil debates! With each group, I learned that I had to adapt to some degree; they often had different assumptions, questions, needs, issues, and language. (I met few self-identified "skeptics" at Muscle Beach, except among the addicts and the beatniks.) I had no prior experience with several of the beach's populations. Fortunately, I was prepared to identify with the muscle crowd; I "clean and jerked" three hundred pounds overhead that summer!

Except for "time-outs" when I did a couple of graduate degrees and when I served in a position with frequent travel, I have exercised with weights and fraternized with fellow sufferers most of the time for six decades. (In a way, I have come full circle. When I was fifteen, they said I was not strong, but I was strong for my age; now, at seventy-eight, they say I am not strong, but I am strong for my age!)

Welcome to the Arnold Fitness Expo

I have spent a lifetime studying fitness, exercise science, and nutrition. As I approached sixty, I decided to deepen and systemize my knowledge. I took a course for fitness trainers from the International Sports Sciences Association (www.issaonline.edu), passed their exam, and became a certified fitness trainer. Nowadays, when I take my annual March pilgrimage to the Arnold Fitness Expo in

---

5. In 1962, my ministry in the weight pen was featured on Art Linkletter's *House Party* television program.

Columbus, Ohio, I approach the guys at the ISSA booth and say, "Hi, remember me? I am your most obscure fitness trainer!" The guys reply, "You must be George!"

A visit to an Arnold Fitness Expo is an experience in hyperbole assault, as signs and barkers from nine hundred tables, booths, and exhibits compete for one's attention. One claims to sell "evolutionary nutrition"; another offers "revolutionary nutrition." One popular table markets "Animal Paks"; another sells "Monster Protein"; another's supplement prepares you for "muscle warfare."

Sometimes the hype engages in a "scientific" spin. You can buy "cellucor" or "musclemed" supplements. One table offered "instant results technology." Another was selling "the world's only stable retox signaling molecule!" (I suppose that may actually mean something, but when I asked the two staff representatives what that meant, they gave two different answers—each as unintelligible as the claim!)

Let's not forget the tables selling T-shirts, sweatshirts, hoodies, and jackets. If you are on a budget, you'll have to choose between "Grizzly Fitness," "Monsta Clothing," "Raging Rhino Sports Apparel," "House of Pain Clothing," and "Intimidation Clothing." You could buy training equipment from the ripped men and women who represented "Iron Rebel Power Gear" or "Rogue Outdoor Power Equipment." I was most amused by T-shirt messages like "Unleash the Beast," "Iron Asylum," "Lift Hard, Die Strong," "Train Like Your Worst Enemy Is Watching," and "Yes I can lift heavy things, No I will not help you move." An occasional T-shirt barks some ideology, such as "The Meek Shall Inherit Nothing!"

There were exceptions to the hype storm. The GNC table only claimed to sell stuff that helps you "live well." The PowerBlock people only claimed to sell "the world's best dumbbell." The International Sports Sciences Association sign read "Creating a Stronger Healthier World." At least several tables featured organizations with explicit Christian identities. At the Flex Performance and Training (www.flexpnt.com) booth, I met the owner—a ripped ex-coach who, past seventy, can do a "for-and-aft split." When I inquired, he shared the story of several experiences, in his sixties, in which he experienced the gift of faith.

The bodybuilding hyperbole merchants can be audacious; they even present hyped claims to people who know better! For instance, the small grandstand now overlooking the Muscle Beach weight pen features an iconic image of "Joe Weider, The Father of Bodybuilding." Weider (the longtime editor of *Muscle and Fitness*) gave the funding for the grandstand. The people who train there know that other notable pioneers—Eugene Sandow, Bernarr McFadden, George Jowett, John Grimek, Jack LaLanne, and others were publicly introducing the fitness and bodybuilding lifestyle years before Weider. Indeed, Bob Hoffman founded the York Barbell Company that marketed barbells, training courses, and food supplements for two decades before Weider surfaced. Hoffman coached the United States's Olympic weightlifting team, was the strongest supporter of the Mr. America contest, and published *Strength and Health* magazine. His company still claims to be, more plausibly, "where it all began."

In time, especially following Hoffman's death in 1985, Weider's juggernaut eclipsed Hoffman's. His magazine eclipsed Hoffman's, his Mr. Olympia contest gained ascendency, and his protégé, Arnold Schwarzenegger, attracted a stampede to all things Weider. But at what cost? Government agencies had to force Weider, multiple times, to drop unwarranted advertising claims supporting supplements and equipment. He (or his staff writers) wrote the "Weider System of Bodybuilding" in which they typically adopted the principles and exercises that others had pioneered—without credits—and attached the Weider name to everything. Furthermore, Weider reigned over the era in which steroid abuse became epidemic in the networks of power lifters and physique contestants. (Following Joe Weider's

50

death in 2013, his successors appeared to distance the company from his excesses; the magazine's tribute article began on page 143.)

The Bodybuilding Culture

It does not require a team of anthropologists and psychologists to identify some of the transparent themes of the muscle crowd culture. In devotees who root their identities in this social world, it is a "macho" culture. Many elite lifters, bodybuilders, and wannabes have embodied some version of this ideal. One who achieves an ideal physique, or who can "bench" big poundage, is to be honored and respected. It is a swaggering, but insecure, self-identity. One's value is measured by one's current bench press or arm size. One must prove oneself to oneself, and to one's peers, almost daily. Bodybuilders can inhabit their gym like alpha dogs; the new guy with wide "lats" can be a threat.

It does not require a mind reader to detect a streak of narcissism in many lifters and bodybuilders. "I look good, therefore I am"; or "I deadlifted double–body weight, therefore I am"; or "I won a trophy, therefore I am."

Bodybuilders, typically, are not avid readers or serious thinkers. They read "inspirational" literature and "self-help" books; they may take a seminar when the latest self-help guru comes to town. They often conceive a self-serving "theology"; the characters in the 2013 film *Pain & Gain* convinced themselves of the credo, "If you believe you deserve it, the universe will serve it!"

This population often lives by an "end justifies the means" ethic, but this is a more recent feature. Once, the subculture's leaders championed the "strength and health" lifestyle; weight training, with a good diet, was nearly the fountain of youth. The field's early

51

role models, like Sandow, LaLanne, and Grimek, were athletic and remarkably healthy.

Some of today's industry leaders still pay lip service to health, and they still market equipment and supplements to people with such goals while, behind the scenes, they enable unhealthy practices that simulate great health while undermining real health. In the 1970s, steroids, human growth hormones, and other "pharmaceuticals" emerged to enhance muscle growth directly, or indirectly—as in accelerating workout recovery. These days, I am told that almost every top-tier competitor is "on the juice."

The trade-off health risks are significant. Every year, one or two well-known physiques die well before his or her time. Many of the current abusers, buffered from the reality of risk by the macho illusion of invincibility, are in denial that what has happened to many others could possibly happen to them. In more sober moments, with near-future goals more important to them than any long-term goals, they accept the possible risks. A title, a trophy, and the attendant self-esteem and prestige seem to be worth a shortened life span. (Some lifters and physique aspirants stop taking the "roids," and probably in time, but often for reasons not necessarily related to health and longevity. One fellow reported, "I gave it up; the stuff was shrinking my privates!")

Some women have bought into the same identity and goals, with similar health risks. Their greater strength and ripped physiques are often accompanied by facial hair and guttural voices. These women, even more than the men, demonstrate what has gone horribly wrong with hard-core bodybuilding.

A half-century ago, the greatest male and female physiques were aesthetic triumphs; today, most people experience the freak physiques as surreal, grotesque. Bodybuilding has become an "extreme sport"; fans pay to see the extreme physiques.

Like almost any subculture, the muscle crowd invents insider humor. The following joke might translate more widely:

A father approached his teenager. "Excuse me, but I suspect that you are on steroids."

"Oh, what gives you that impression, Dad?"

"Well, three things. First, your voice sounds like Darth Vader. Second, Mom says that you shave your back every week. Third, you are my daughter, for crying out loud!"

In even the most hard-core gyms, however, you will find some heterogeneity. Quite a few power lifters and biceps-flexors are on the juice, but the Olympic lifters are probably not, nor are many of the people who work out there for the "blue-collar gym ambiance" or the lower monthly fee.

Meanwhile, the majority population you'd observe in a typical health club will not reflect this profile, for one simple reason: this is not where they primarily ground their identity. The population you see on the weight machines, stair climbers, and treadmills may be as heterogeneous as you'd find at any location in the entire city. The "New-Year's-resolutioners" are there for a while each year; perhaps 20 percent stick with the fitness lifestyle past April. One observes a range of people who have a primary sport interest other than weight training; off-season basketball players, weekend tennis players, tri-athletes, and others have added resistance training to their regimen.

One can often observe driven, addictive people who have traded a destructive addiction for a "positive addiction." (These people inspire me. We may have no idea of the demons that some of them are overcoming.) The biggest single change in a health club's clientele since the 1950s is the increased number of medical, legal, education, business, and other professionals who now train.

I will not attempt to catalogue a health club's entire membership. Even some of the gym's best-built people have little interest in how much they can deadlift and no interest in posing before an audience of strangers to compete for a thirty-dollar trophy.

Profiling the Atheists I Have Met

In gyms and health clubs, I have met confessing atheists and have valued conversations with professed atheists ever since. Over the years, I've engaged in more than a hundred extended conversations, somewhat more often in recent years than before and more in e-mail conversations than before, and more among the mentalists than among the muscle crowd. However, I first met most of the features of atheists in gyms and, since the next chapter is longer than this one, let me feature them here. (Some atheists reflect more than one of the features below, occasionally several. Since most of these features [e.g., egotism or narcissism or belonging to a group] are evident in the traits of Christians too, I am not totally describing the causes of belief or unbelief. Rather I am observing spiritual, emotional, ethical, and physical factors that contribute to, or coexist with, denial of belief in God.)

1. Some atheist friends reached this important conclusion while teenagers. (They were rebellious, they enjoyed shocking their elders, and when profanity lost its zing, professing atheism could consistently provoke adult discomfort. In conversations, they typically want one to know what precocious children they were!)

2. Some atheists (and Christians) I have known are exceptionally proud, even egotistical or narcissistic, people. (*Pride* is, of course, the core driving force among the "Seven Deadly Sins"). So, say, if they concluded in their teen years that there is no God, they could not possibly have been wrong on something this important (even if they have changed their minds on many other matters).

3. Intellectual arrogance functions so much like pride that I was tempted to list them together. But some of the nicest people assume that their opinions in many matters are infallible. In one recent period, I was in conversation with an architect, an electrical engineer, and a social psychologist. They discovered that their field was more complex than they had imagined at first, in ways beyond what they once could have imagined. Yet it had not occurred to them that people who study *any* serious field discover unanticipated complexity. So in fields of some interest beyond their specialty, like philosophy, theology, or cosmology, they had connected the few dots they saw, formed a conclusion, and became yet another instance of Alexander Pope's observation, "A little knowledge is a dangerous thing."

4. Many atheists have reflected on experiences around fathers who were weak, absent, neglectful, or abusive.[6]

5. As the previous point suggests, much atheism is more emotionally than intellectually driven; chief among the emotional drivers of atheism is *anger*.[7]

6. Many atheists are members of affinity groups or subcultures in which atheism is a core nonnegotiable belief within the subculture's worldview; belonging is contingent upon agreeing.

7. Some atheists were (perhaps unconsciously) socialized into

---

6.   Paul C. Vitz, an extensively published PhD psychologist who was once an atheist and is now a Roman Catholic Christian, studied the lives of notable atheists, and documented this remarkable correlation in *Faith of the Fatherless: The Psychology of Atheism*, second edition (San Francisco: Ignatius Press, 2013). Vitz demonstrates that this correlation at least partly accounts for many more atheists than I had perceived.

7.   Peter Hitchens, brother of the famous late atheist Christopher Hitchens and once an atheist himself before converting to Anglican Christianity, has reflected on the role that anger played in his own atheism and in the lives of most of the atheists he has known. See his book *The Rage Against God: How Atheism Led Me to Faith* (Grand Rapids: Zondervan, 2010).

the "philosophical materialism" that in the nineteenth century became the assumed worldview of much of the Western academy.[8] This view assumes that matter is all there is; *nothing*, therefore, could possibly exist behind or beyond matter.

8. A negative image of the church or its history[9] or its leaders has influenced some people toward, or into, atheism. In recent years, some people experienced the Roman Catholic pedophile priest scandal as "the last straw."

9. Some people have adopted atheism because they want to live by their own agenda and, therefore, do not want to answer to a deity. Mortimer Adler famously declared, "I want atheism to be true." Dostoyevsky observed, "If God is dead, then everything is permitted."

10. When "the New Atheism" became fashionable in the first decade of this century, it became widely suggested that, when one becomes an atheist, one joins the ranks of the "Brights." I have visited with at least a dozen average achievers who had quickly accepted the offer of a superior status.

11. Many people who disbelieve are or have been at some stage of chemical dependency. Addiction is a "complete" disease that affects the whole person—spiritual, emotional, mental, and physical—typically in that order; recovery typically happens in reverse order. As a drug gradually hijacks a person's life, spirituality is generally first to go and last to return. On a scale of one to ten, many people never become down-and-out level-ten addicts. I have met people at (say) level four who are "white knuckling" their way through an apparently successful life; their mental and physical capacities are less affected, but their spirits are incapacitated and their emo-

---

8. See Sheldrake, *Science Set Free*.
9. The church history they "know" is usually much more fiction than fact. Their sources are usually their grapevine, or atheist debunkers like Richard Dawkins or Christopher Hitchins—who selectively draw from history, real or imagined, in the service of propaganda.

tional life is compromised. Their drug(s), often with their music or their companions, fill their spiritual and emotional life synthetically.[10]

12. Some people's belief in transcendence is volatile or cyclic; they believed last year but not this year; or last year they were atheists, now they are "into" Zen Buddhism.

I have discovered the rather obvious insight that, of course, not all atheists are the same. Each person has a distinct personality, set of life experiences, and so on. Furthermore, not all "atheisms" are the same; atheists can, and do, disagree with each other.[11]

I have often asked professing atheists to describe the kind of God they have difficulty believing in. Typically, I get one of two kinds of answers.

People influenced by philosophical materialism do not believe in the possibility of a God because they believe that nothing of any significance exists beyond the material world. So I may ask about their relationship with their spouse or their child, or the book or movie or music that most moved them, as an honest wedge to look beyond matter for meaning.

Some people, on the other hand, start describing the "god" they reject. While their descriptions can vary (the "old man in the sky" can still show up), I can always identify with them; I could not believe in that kind of "god" either. If they are sufficiently open, we talk about the Christian understanding of God. I often speak from material in Luke's Gospel, very often from chapter 15.

10. For a summary of addiction theory and the church's role in recovery, see my *Radical Outreach: The Recovery of Apostolic Ministry and Evangelism* (Nashville: Abingdon, 2003), chapter 5.
11. Nick Spencer's *Atheists: The Origin of the Species* (London: Bloomsbury, 2013) explains, in the first chapter, that atheism took multiple forms almost from the beginning. The book is a useful history of atheism's development in the West.

Ten Principles for Presence in Affinity Groups

Let me report more broadly on my participant-observer role, as a Christian, with the muscle crowd (which I have continued with the mentalists), which would apply to becoming involved with any subculture or interest group.

The "participant" part of such a role is indispensable. One should be interested in what they do. (So don't join a stamp club or a biker club if you are "not into" stamps or motorcycles. "Flex" with your interests!) One should do what they do, and be sufficiently knowledgeable and competent—or obviously seeking the knowledge and competence.

So with the exception of guys training for contests, I train about as seriously as anyone else in the gym. And I have enough knowledge of physiology and training lore to give feedback and talk shop. I have observed that serious gym-devotees have little respect for people who never break a sweat and only go through the motions, or who talk or text on their cell phones from a machine that someone else needs to use. A fairly high level of knowledge and participation is necessary to be credible. Then find some people you like, get in conversation, enjoy their company, learn from them.

What is one's role as a Christian in such a subculture? I can only answer for myself, in part because I am also a Methodist clergyman and an academic, but my answer may help others to answer for themselves. I gravitated toward the model reflected in the ministry of Jesus and his disciples among the people of Galilee, and especially Jesus's presence at a wedding in Cana. He attended primarily to celebrate the wedding with the people, but when a need for ministry surfaced, he responded.

Gradually, I developed the following policies as a Christian among the muscle crowd and the mentalists:

1. I usually initiate conversations with people; I now identify myself as a grandpa and a retired dean and professor from a divinity school, still learning about (say) exercise physiology or reading body language.

2. In the matters of faith, I usually respond to their questions. After some time, I might invite any questions they have, or I might share something from a Christian worldview—like how we view something in the news related to (say) addiction, race relations, or war.

3. In such ministry of conversation, I do more listening than talking; in many conversations, I spend at least 80 percent of the time listening.

4. When I am saying something, I often can affirm something they said and build on that. I usually engage in the ministry of explanation. In conversation with secular seekers, we spend much of our lives explaining what Christianity is basically about; what it claims, teaches, offers, and calls us to; and what it is like to live by it—rather than what they and their peers have assumed about it.

5. I often identify with them as a "fellow skeptic!" In my doctoral work in communication studies, I was impressed by the views of the ancient Greek sophist Gorgias—who, among other things, concluded that reality is too complex and impenetrable for us to understand it. Something deep within me agreed; every field I have studied was more complex than I had imagined, in ways I could not have imagined. So, we would never know the truth about ultimate reality if it had not been revealed. Even those of us who have discovered (or been discovered by) that revelation admit that, in Paul's words, "We know in part";

59

the lens we are given in revelation lets us perceive reality "as through a dark glass."

6. *If* I engage in any "apologetics," I do not usually present an "argument." I simply engage in theological reflection in conversation with someone who has some questions!

7. I have learned more useful theology, in reflecting on the questions secular people sometimes ask, than one could probably learn in an entire degree program in "desk theology."

8. As Jesus modeled at the wedding in Cana, if the need arises I respond in ministry. I have helped people with anxiety, identity, and self-esteem issues, through loss and grief, marital and vocational decisions, and the decision to follow Christ.

9. I remind myself, often, that they matter to God and it is important for Christians to love them unconditionally and to believe in what they can become.

10. Occasionally, they kind of make me their pastor!

Chapter Four

Sojourning with the Mentalists

I have now been involved with the populations who inhabit health clubs for the better part of a lifetime. Even in the 1950s, almost half of the people in such gyms had no serious Christian background, memory, or identity. Since then, their numbers have grown, and they are the large majority in almost any health club today. Even today, however, not many people who pump iron are self-identified, card-carrying, vocal "skeptics"; but many self-avowed skeptics populate my other affinity group of "mentalists."

Doubt, of course, has long been with us; most medieval villages had their pet atheist![1] In the West, every generation has known vocal skeptics; but there are more of them now, and more in some populations than others. So, some ethnic populations are more secular than others; one meets more Jewish skeptics than Irish skeptics. Some vocational populations are more secular than others; one meets more skeptical engineers than skeptical nurses.

Many entertainers seem to be secular, amoral, inwardly tortured, skeptical souls, but even entertainers are not created equal;

---

1. Nick Spencer's *Atheists: The Origin of the Species* (London: Bloomsbury, 2014) is an interesting history of "atheisms" (plural) in the West.

musicians, broadcasters, and actors are best understood within their own micro-cultures. Mentalists constitute one of many species in the entertainment world. They "read minds" for the enjoyment of the audience. (A small minority are "psychics"—who perform Halloween magic!)

How I Became a "Mentalist"

Let me tell you how I gradually discovered this fraternity. Like many kids, I was once into magic—the theatrical art of illusion. On Saturday mornings, I often helped the two guys open up at the Jahn the Magic Man shop in downtown Miami. I never sawed, impaled, or levitated anyone, but I learned to vanish a coin, and turn a blue silk to red, and move a ball from under one cup to another, then transform the ball into a tangerine. In time, the magic props were forgotten in a drawer. Then, seven years ago (and over five decades later), a friend invited me to a meeting of the local magic club in Lexington, Kentucky. I caught the fever again, but this time around it was mental magic; I became a mentalist.

What is a *mentalist*? The popular CBS TV program *The Mentalist* opened with a definition: "Someone who uses mental acuity, hypnosis, and/or suggestion. A master manipulator of thoughts and behavior." The lead character, Patrick Jane, was once a performing "mind reader" and "psychic" who became a consultant for the California Bureau of Investigation, and later for the FBI. Through astute observation and intuition, this postmodern Sherlock discovered who is guilty; then his team gathered the evidence to prove it. If time was short, however, the suspect confessed in response to Patrick Jane's clever bluff or shrewd probing!

Most mentalists are not crime-solvers; they perform for people's entertainment. They perform "effects" or "demonstrations" (*not* "tricks")! The basic theme is "the power of the mind." The mentalist may engage in "cold reading"—as in knowing things about the person they are "reading." Or the mentalist may know what someone is thinking, or influence their thoughts or choices, or predict a near-future event, or move an object through mental force. Some mentalists may also demonstrate remarkable calculation or memory powers; or they may hypnotize several spectators. (A British mentalist of the mid-twentieth century, Maurice Fogel, used to hypnotize a goose!) Increasingly, performers (like me) make it less about the performer and more about spectators experiencing their own mental capacities.

More specifically, a mentalist may have a spectator open a book at random and tell her a word, or a thought, or a scene on the page; or invite the spectator to draw something, and then duplicate it while standing across the stage; or hand the spectator a combination lock and then influence the spectator to the combination that opens it; or ask the spectator to silently recall a friend's name from elementary school and then tell her the name. The mentalist may have several people each place a personal item into a cloth bag and then discern which object belongs to which person, while revealing something about each owner. Or the mentalist may tell the spectator which of her hands holds the coin, or what playing card she thought of. The range of mentalism effects is extensive; no performer masters and performs everything.

Learning from the Skeptics

So, that is how I became a hobbyist mentalist, and that is what mentalism is about.

One day, in an e-mail exchange with a British mentalist, I mentioned that several of the mentalists I had met seemed to be skeptics, or agnostics, or even atheists. He wrote back, "Most of the magicians and mentalists that I know are atheists." I gradually discovered that my hobbyist interest in mentalism had led me into one of the more skeptical subcultures in our galaxy! Since then, I have interviewed mentalists, spent time with mentalists, attended their annual convention in Las Vegas, read their sources and their discussions on Internet forums, and exchanged e-mails and phone calls. I enjoy these people and I learn from them.

What could a Christian leader learn from skeptical mentalists? Consider two answers.

One lesson recalls that the best actors identify with, and "become," their character in the play or film; the lesson acknowledges that mentalists are actors too.[2] In performance magic, including mentalism, some "theatrical deception" may be involved; but this is not unique to magic. Theatrical deception is involved in a wide range of performing arts; audiences, by suspending their disbelief, buy into the deception and sometimes experience "magic." A generation ago, when I saw Paul Scofield playing King Lear in Stratford Upon Avon's Royal Shakespearian Theater, I "experienced" the death of a great king. What made the scene so believable? Scofield so identified with the Lear role and character, that he virtually believed that he was Lear, and was experiencing Lear's death.

In most performing arts, including public speaking, the most important factor in performance is deeply experiencing the meaning of what one is presenting as one performs. So, as an actor, the effective mentalist "believes" and "experiences" the magic as the audience is experiencing it, and that, more than anything else, makes the effect believable.

Compared to effective mentalists and other actors, the minds of many Christian presenters of revealed truth seem to be somewhere

---

2. Robert Houdin, a nineteenth-century European magician famously commented, "A magician is an actor playing the part of a magician." Likewise, a mentalist is an actor playing the part of a mentalist.

else in the moment of speaking; the result is a spoken message with the authenticity removed.

The second lesson was stimulated by a thread on a "Magic Café" website, which posed this question to mentalists: Who would you rather perform for—people who really believe in ESP and the paranormal and so on, or for skeptics? Every mentalist who participated in the discussion said that he or she would rather engage skeptics than "believers." Several mentalists experienced credulous audiences as "boring"; they wished they could perform *only* for skeptics. One mentalist reveled in the recent moment when, after he apparently read a skeptic's very thoughts, the skeptic commented, "Okayyy.... I am officially weirded out!"

In most of the circled-wagon churches I have observed, the leaders would far rather fraternize with the saints and preach to the choir than *ever* engage skeptics, especially beyond the church, on secular turf.

The Roots of Skepticism in the Mentalism Ranks

I discovered that the British mentalist's e-mail message was accurate. While most hobbyist mentalists (like me) fit our society's demographic range, many professional (and other more serious) mentalists are skeptics, agnostics, or atheists. One reason is not unique: Like many serious subcultures, this peer group almost requires ideological conformity to belong (with just enough exceptions to "prove" they are "tolerant")! However, this community experiences some distinct roots that shape their worldview.

First, while many secular people still have a "church background," and ancestors who were confessing Christians, the (Halloween magic) "psychic's" perspective is rooted in an alternative spirituality—the "spiritualism" that reaches back as deep as the 1500s and thrived in the English-speaking world and much of Europe from the 1840s through the 1920s. Spiritualists generally believed in a God—defined as "infinite intelligence," with no serious Christology and little reference to scripture. Spiritualists believed that people who died became "discarnate souls" who now lived in a spirit world, who could still communicate with people in this material world—through a gifted "medium," during a "séance."

Even today, a psychic's (or bizarrist's) effects may include spirit "visitations"—expressed as a "spirit bell" ringing or "spirit writing" on a slate. Some psychic performers today no longer actually believe in spiritualism, but others tell me that they do believe in the spirit world and in the forces that their performances represent. Since the forces are not controllable or predictable, however, at least some of a performance relies upon theatrical deception. If they are aware of any Christian ancestors, that is less relevant than for most other secular people. Their paradigm of transcendence is different; their worldview frames reality in a different way.

Psychics do not always take themselves, or their views, too seriously. Their Internet conversations frequently feature jokes. The following riddle is my favorite:

Q: When a midget psychic escaped the penitentiary, how did the headline read?
A: "Small Medium at Large"

Second, the more psychological mentalists (the large majority) also have historical roots apart from Christianity. One such source is the extra-sensory perception (ESP) research that began in England in the late nineteenth century and in the United States in the 1930s, at the J. B. Rhine Institute at Duke University. Rhine, a PhD botanist who became a psychologist, wanted to know if human beings have a "sixth sense" that makes possible mind-to-mind communication without involving the five acknowledged senses. He discovered that five visual symbols—a circle, a cross, three wavy lines, a square, and a star—could often catalyze mind-to-mind "telepathy."

A typical ESP experiment involved a shuffled deck of twenty-five ESP cards—with five each of the five symbols. As the tester dealt each card, he or she visualized it; the experimental subject, on the other side of a screen, attempted to intuit which symbol was dealt. The odds of being right, of course, were one in five, 20 percent. Many experiments produced positive-but-weak results; occasional subjects "hit" in the high twenties and several in the high thirties—suggesting a sixth sense in at least some people. (One subject scored twenty-one "hits" in a run of twenty-five cards, several times; he typically scored near 40 percent, and he exhibited extraordinary awareness his whole life.) More recent research reports that people who believe in ESP typically score higher than 20 percent; skeptics typically score lower than 20 percent!

Most mentalists today perform some effects with ESP cards, or they read "body language," or (most often) they perform demonstrations of mind-to-mind influence. Their approach is more "psychological" than the psychic's. Many mentalists consider themselves rooted in psychology and "science" more generally; some are (self-designated) "philosophical materialists" who do not believe in the existence of anything beyond what the five senses can perceive. Most mentalists make no claim of possessing extraordinary mental powers; nor (since audiences make up their own minds anyway) do they *dis*claim such powers.

Meanwhile, the Rhine Institute has moved in a very different direction. It has expanded its explorations into virtually the whole realm of "paranormal" realities and alternative spiritualities. The institute now promotes interest in actual telepathy, clairvoyance, precognition, and psychokinesis, as well as human-animal communication, and the survival of human consciousness after death. The institute's parade of seminar leaders report research and views on such topics as remote viewing, esoteric healing, deja vu experiences, channeling, dreams, ghosts, poltergeists, and haunting experiences. While the Institute's agenda was once largely confined to the original ESP research, today their openness to the transcendent now includes astrology, Hinduism, shamanism, yoga, and other metaphysical worldviews. They now seem to believe, or be open to, almost everything except Christianity!

More Roots of Skepticism

I have discovered some other factors that help to account for the range of skepticism within the mentalism subculture.

For instance, I have met at least a dozen secular mentalists who are ethnically Jewish. The extensive secularization of Jewish populations is one of the major unwritten chapters in the history of Western secularization. One mentalist reports that he was raised in a home of nonpracticing Jews. As a teenager, he thought of himself as agnostic. Now, as an adult with a family, he tells me he is probably an atheist, certainly a materialist. He is not sure how he arrived to this point; it did not happen consciously or by decision. Although the details vary enormously, his experience is similar to a majority of the Jewish mentalists I have visited with. However, a significant minority of Jewish mentalists are devout practicing Jews.

A fair number of mentalists in North America and Europe are widely rumored to be homosexual. I have not interviewed any of them specifically about this, but I have interviewed some of their colleagues. Since most churches cannot affirm this part of their lifestyle, this supplies an apparent reason to believe that Christianity could not possibly be true. (They are not the first cohort population to assume that something that seems so right to them could possibly be in contrast to God's will.)

Many mentalists of recent history, like many other entertainers, proved to be self-absorbed, troubled, out-of-control souls. The two most prominent early–twentieth century mentalists serve as cases.

For instance, the subtitle of the biography of Claude Alexander Conlin features him as "Mindreader, Charlatan, Extortionist, Bootlegger, Bigamist, Murderer, Magician!" The biography tells us that America's most popular mind reader, even off-stage, "was one of the most charismatic charlatans who ever lived. He played most of every aspect of his life for his own advantage, forsaking a string of wives, lovers and friends in the process."[3] He sometimes passed himself off as a minister of a "Spiritual Church," credentialed by a mail-order ordination certificate! He also passed himself off as a counseling psychologist, and even published a five-volume course, "The Inner Secrets of Psychology."

Mel Gordon's biography of Erik Jan Hanussen,[4] a mentalist in Germany's Third Reich era, profiles an even more complex character. "Hanussen" was the last of his several aliases and, escaping from his ethnic Jewish roots, reflected the last of his several reinvented identities. He joined a circus as a boy and was socialized into the "carney" worldview; from that experience, Gordon tells us, "the good, the sacred, the nonsexual did not exist. Erik Jan Hanussen was being born."[5]

As a magician, clairvoyant, thought-reader, hypnotist, astrologer, forecaster, and psychic detective, Hanussen performed across much of Europe before settling in Germany to take advantage of Germany's then-current fascination with the occult. He could find a

---

3. David Charvet, *Alexander: The Man Who Knows*, expanded edition (Pasadena, CA: Mike Caveney's Magic Words, 2007), 17.

4. Mel Gordon, *Eric Jan Hanussen: Hitler's Jewish Clairvoyant* (Los Angeles: Feral House, 2001).

5. Ibid., 12.

needle hidden in an auditorium. He predicted many major events in the history of his time (although some predictions did not materialize). He apparently believed in occult supernatural forces, but his performances relied on deception; through nonverbal cues, his confederates in the auditorium could communicate over three hundred messages to him. In time, he published a tabloid and a magazine. He became an astrology guru.

Germany's rich and famous flocked to Hanussen's séances. He apparently coached Adolph Hitler in public speaking and in the staging of large-scale public theater. He stunned Germany by predicting, from astrological signs, that Hitler was destined to become Germany's leader—which may have functioned as a self-fulfilling prophesy. He became a confidante of the Third Reich, but he was assassinated when Gestapo thugs (who owed him money) decided that the mind reader knew too much!

The twentieth century's most notable mentalist-writers were also troubled. Theodore Anneman, who published *Practical Mental Magic* in 1944, was one of the three literary founders of modern mentalism; he was brilliant, but he fought low self-esteem, depression, alcoholism, and other inner demons and died by his own hand at thirty-four. Tony Corinda, who published *13 Steps to Mentalism* in 1968, became a total recluse for many years, until his death in 2010. T. A. Waters published *Mind, Myth and Magic* in 1993; his friends observed him spending his last years in reclusion, addicted to peanut butter sandwiches, before dying at sixty.

Such tragic stories continue. In one month, a well-known Canadian mentalist was convicted of sexually assaulting a minor, and a well-known American performer—struggling with depression and other health issues, and a separation from his wife, died by his own hand.

Many performers are charming, engaging, confident public personalities, but underneath the appearance (as Chesterton observed), "the wildness lies in wait."[6]

Five Noted Skeptics

We can characterize the secularity that pervades much of mentalism in more recent history by profiling five leaders.

Today, England's Derren Brown is perhaps the world's best-known performing mentalist, and he freely confesses atheism. His book[7] partially reveals how he came to this point. He was raised in a Pentecostal Fundamentalist church in England. As a boy, he believed in "God, Jesus, and the Devil"; he assumes that what his church taught accurately and fully represented Christianity. While a student at the University of Bristol, he experimented with a Ouija board. His Christian friends warned him that the "planchette" moves because of demonic forces. Brown knew, however, that the planchette moves from a natural cause—when people expect and will the glass to move, their subconscious "ideomotor" activity moves the body's muscles to move the planchette. So Brown decided that Christians did not know what they were talking about. He was later told that the Bible is not reliable history, and he also met Richard Dawkins and other atheists who confirmed those ideas for him.

Brown is heavily into some of the themes of modernity—evidence, logic, and especially science. He assures us that science cannot *yet* explain everything, but it will. He assures us that the march of scientific discovery is "rational" and "cumulative," but he did not study science at the University of Bristol, and his claim about

---

6. G. K. Chesterton, *Orthodoxy*, 72 (e-book edition). Chesterton's point was that the world is not as *logical* as it appears, but the punchline applies here as well.

7. Derren Brown, *Tricks of the Mind* (London: Random House, 2007).

71

science's cumulative progress reveals his unfamiliarity with science's actual history.[8]

Brown spends energy defending science against the challenges of "multiculturalism" and other threats from postmodernity. As a defender of establishment science, he dismisses all "alternative medicines" with a sweep of the hand—including acupuncture and chiropractic. He squeezes Christianity, other religions, the paranormal, and all other "superstitions" into the same category. Then, he assumes, if you can expose one "superstition" in any one of them as ludicrous—such as an alleged ancient Aztec religious practice of sacrificing one person each day so the sun would rise the next day—you have logically destroyed all "superstitions," including Christianity.

While Derren Brown is a skeptic in his worldview, the public role he has chosen reveals that he has joined recent history's parade of public "debunkers"—who make headlines, and gain notoriety (and wealth), by "exposing" and mocking ideas, practices, and people they disagree with. Consider the interesting fraternity he has joined.

Harry Houdini initially won fame as an escape artist; but he remained famous as a debunker. For years, he discredited one spiritualist, psychic, or medium after another. He claimed that they were all frauds—except him! He promised that, after he died, he would communicate with the living. Annual Houdini séances are conducted, on the anniversary of his death, to this day.

Martin Gardner was a journalist who specialized in mathematics and science topics. He was a smorgasbord debunker; his pen attacked the Bible, creationism, parapsychology, Scientology, Christian

8. Thomas Kuhn, in *The Structure of Scientific Revolutions* (Chicago: University of Chicago Press, 1962), explained that most significant advances in scientific understanding are *not* cumulative, nor are they rooted in rational thought alone. Rather, most major scientific advances come from "paradigm shifts"; the source of such a shift is typically more intuitive than logical, is typically *dis*continuous with the prevailing scientific wisdom, and the scientific establishment often fights the new paradigm, sometimes for years, before they can even physically perceive the new evidence!

Science, UFOs, and much more. Philosophically, he was a deist who loved the line attributed to G. K. Chesterton: "[To an atheist] the universe is the most exquisite masterpiece ever constructed by nobody!"

James "The Amazing" Randi has devoted much of his life to exposing faith healers and the entire range of paranormal claims and practices. Randi calls himself an "investigator" whose objectivity might be suspect when one realizes that his "investigations," for over four decades, have *always* discovered what he expected, and wanted, to find! His self-image and flamboyant approach are reflected in the title of his well-known essay "Why I Deny Religion, How Silly and Fantastic It Is, and Why I'm a Dedicated and Vociferous Bright."

In recent years, Penn Jillette (of the amusing Penn and Teller magic team) has exceeded Randi's "vociferousity." His weekly "documentary" show aired on the Showtime cable channel for eight years. As viewed through his three lenses—naturalist, libertarian, and capitalist—the entire range of claims regarding religion, the supernatural, and the paranormal, as well as environmentalism, alternative medicines, anti-smoking laws, and most other government health regulations are all "crap."

While we could add other colorful personalities to that parade, some patterns already emerge. The five are bright, clever, articulate, and even charming bluffers, but they are not intellectual heavyweights; there are two known undergraduate college degrees among the five, and what they palm off as "research" is an embarrassment to the academy. Debunkers seem to read a lot, but on complex matters in regard to history, science, religion, or philosophy they are allergic to the writings of real historian, scientists, theologians, and philosophers; with the exception of Gardner, they typically read and consult with other skeptics and debunkers.

Eugene Burger (the leading philosopher in magic) once told me that debunkers are "fundamentalists turned inside out!" Their dogmatic confidence in all of their own conclusions, in the entire range of complex issues, matches any of the narrowest ideologues they detest. In seizing on the worst single example of "religion" (or any other "myth") they can find, and then screaming that it's *all* like that, they indulge in more extravagant stereotyping than any racist ever considered. Their aversion to facts, evidence, and authorities, and their preference for misrepresentation, scorn, and ridicule, may exceed any and all of the fundamentalisms they loathe. Still, they are bush league: historically, they pale in comparison to the propaganda force of the Third Reich or Stalinism (or the NRA!).

Folk Skepticism

For most people, including debunkers, their socialization, experiences, and education shape and script their view of ultimate reality; unfiltered objectivity is rare, perhaps nonexistent. So some engineers interpret the whole cosmos as mechanical, while some physicists believe their field will one day explain everything—if it doesn't already! Likewise, some magicians (including psychics and mentalists) who read, think, and perform magic; and watch magic videos; and attend magic clubs and magic conventions; and fraternize with other magicians, tend to see reality through a magician's paradigm. They know, from learning and experience, how easy it is to "misdirect" people's attention and to deceive people in many ways. Then they observe physicians prescribing placebos, the blatant deception in much advertising, and politicians oversimplifying the issues and promising what cannot be delivered—and getting elected, and they conclude that it is *all* theatrical illusion.

They may use the magic paradigm to "explain" (or explain away) Christianity. So when they read of Moses turning his staff into a snake, they know how a magician *could* produce such an effect; with several such examples, they leap to the assumption that *all* of the miracles in scripture and in subsequent history are mere tricks. Or they may read about Jesus's conversation with the Samaritan woman in John 4 as a demonstration of "cold reading," and be oblivious to his greater significance.

Many mentalists started out as magicians, and their specific experience seems to have affected their assumptions about reality. Two mentalists, for instance, spent time as house magicians in strip clubs. The experience seems to have shaped them in several ways. For instance, they gained experience performing for people who did not really show up to see their kind of entertainment! More to the point, there seems to be some residual shame attached, which is compensated for by hyper-righteousness (and self-righteousness) in some other area of life.

So one marketer of mentalism effects and props takes pride in his responsive and honest customer service, and he expresses contempt for other merchants who, in his view, do not conform to his moral code. He feels morally indignant toward "religion," because "religion has started so many wars." I was astonished that an elementary fact had escaped my friend's notice: that the propaganda of kings, tyrants, generals, politicians, and their spinmeisters has often "misdirected" the people, and the historians; for instance, most of the "wars of religion" weren't really about religion at all! Nor had he recalled the role of atheist-dictators in the twentieth century's mammoth wars, concentration camps, and genocides.

It would be possible, of course, to exaggerate the extent to which mentalists are different from other people, or different from the church's people. During the lunch break on the last day of a mentalism convention, one fellow asked what I do for a living. I replied that I am a retired theologian who still does some writing and speaking. He kind of bristled and said, "I am an orthodox atheist!" My response, a tongue-in-cheek question, confused him: "What would a heretical atheist believe, or not believe?" When the bell rang for the first afternoon session, I unilaterally sat next to him.

Following the next break, I returned to what I thought was the chair I had occupied next to his, but I mistakenly sat in his chair. When he returned, the look on his face was the same as I have observed in churches when a member discovered someone occupying their pew! We did manage to converse some before the session began. He recalled, with some intensity, a time when a "gospel magician" announced that his way to perform the famous "Magic Square" effect was "God's way." My new acquaintance said he found that claim to be "arrogant, absolutely arrogant." I found it useful to agree: "Actually, it was worse than arrogant." As that last session concluded, he mumbled, "See you next year?" The next year, we joined up for dinner and conversation. When he asked a question about the four Gospels, our conversation took a significant turn. We now exchange e-mails.

Like many public performers who are bright and who receive adulation, it does not take a Cold Reader to perceive an astonishing level of pride and arrogance in the personalities of some mentalists. I have interviewed mentalists who consider themselves experts on everything, who pontificate on anything. I interviewed a bright younger mentalist with skills in suggestion, including hypnotism. When he studied psychology at a state university, he discovered that, as a trained mentalist, he knew some things that his psychology professor did not know. He said to his professor, "I can make you forget your name"; then, to the professor's astonishment, he proceeded to do it! By the time the young mentalist had processed the experience of proving he knew something his professor did not, he had decided that he probably knew *more* than the professor, and probably more than the whole faculty—so he "obviously" did not need to study beyond his bachelor's degree!

The skepticism in many mentalists is often emotionally driven—typically rooted in experiences during their childhood or youth. Usually, when I am interviewing a mentalist-skeptic and I ask them about their view of the Christian faith and how they acquired that view, they respond emotionally at first—often defensively, often in anger. They usually know little or nothing about serious Christianity, they are badly misinformed, and they typically bring the memories of alienating experiences to such a discussion. They may report being raised in a "dysfunctional" religious family, or life with an abusive religious parent or uncle, or the "nun from hell" who was their sixth-grade teacher. Often, what they perceived as self-righteous, judgmental, and bigoted fundamentalists, who (they assumed) represented the whole of Christianity, turned them off at an intensity level that stuck.

Most people's view of reality is the "socially constructed" view of a community or an affinity group, and one's membership is contingent upon sharing the community's core beliefs and values; to be included, one agrees. Some mentalists are like this, but more so. Visiting over lunch, for instance, a well-known mentalist said that he is an agnostic. When I asked him to help me understand that, he replied that he studied at Cornell University. "So," he reported, "I am agnostic."

I confessed that I did not see the connection. He reported that, in the time he studied at Cornell, the astro-physicist Carl Sagan was the Cornell faculty's biggest star. He quoted Sagan as declaring, "The idea that God is an oversized white male with a flowing beard who sits in the sky and tallies the fall of every sparrow is ludicrous." He added that Sagan did not feel he knew enough to be an atheist, so he said he was an agnostic.

Then I made the connection: my conversation partner was inferring that if you were a *real* Cornell man, you *would* be an agnostic, like Carl Sagan. Group loyalty can impact one's worldview and identity, subtly but profoundly. (In almost all of my interviews with mentalist-skeptics, the picture of the "god" they reject is a cartoon caricature—more or less like Sagan's.)

On the public scene, magic and mentalism feature their fair share of self-assured, dogmatic, in-your-face "evangelists" for agnosticism and atheism. I have interviewed several; they assume that they know the truth regarding all of the questions and issues that theologians, philosophers, and ethicists have struggled with for centuries! On the mega-issue of suffering, for instance, one fellow could not recall anything he had ever read on the subject, but he knew the answers! It doesn't take a mind reader to detect the immaturity, self-absorption, narcissism, and self-aggrandizement that drive some of the public magicians. Derren Brown, the Amazing Randi, and Penn Jillette function with the confidence of papal infallibility on every topic; Gillette can publicly, and savagely, ridicule Christians—especially Roman Catholics.

Some mentalists are not opposed to Christianity, nor are they "agnostics." They are "ignostics." They are ignorant of basic Christianity, they have little-to-no faithful information for a Christian advocate to build on, and they have false information to unlearn. They are fairly typical secular people, who may be vaguely familiar with several of the Ten Commandments and unfamiliar with the Lord's Prayer. One mentalist asked me what I do for a living; I said I teach in a divinity school. He asked what else I do; I said I occasionally give lectures at other educational institutions—like at Biola University the month before. He asked, "What did you lecture on?" I said, "The Communication of Christianity." He asked, "What was it about—religion?" (Welcome to "ignosticism"!)

Many of the mentalists I have interviewed are almost as "ignostic." Mentalism, like much of the entertainment world, functions without much regard to Christianity. But the field still draws imaginative metaphors and allusions from Christianity. For instance, the community is fascinated with the quest for an ideal blockbuster mentalism effect that has been approximated but never perfected. Wouldn't it be wonderful, mentalists dream, if you could invite a spectator to name a number from one to fifty-two, and then name any card in a card deck—and, bam, the Jack of Spades is, indeed, the ninth card down? This mythical effect is known as "any card at any number," or ACAAN. That one idealized effect is the Holy Grail of mentalism.

Are there theists, and even Christians, in the mentalism community? Yes (though more among the hobbyists than the vocational performers), and others are friendly, or believers, if not committed. But not all of the "believers" are advocates, or even assets to the Christian movement. In my conversations, perhaps a third of the mentalism convention attendees were raised in churches, and they retain some of the faith of their childhood, and perhaps half still attend; they are amused, and not threatened, by the skeptics, but they do not engage them. One self-avowed theist had nevertheless rejected "organized religion"; he said he had "made up my own religion!"

One well-known public mentalist presents a case study that no fiction writer could invent. He reports that he believes in God and is "spiritual," and he ridicules and makes fun of his atheist friends. But he is widely rumored to be a "womanizer," and his professed lifestyle would embarrass an alley cat. In a public presentation, he said that passing off the séances he leads as "real contacts with the dead" is morally justified because "I have an expensive lifestyle, so I do whatever I have to do to support it." He joked that he knew another mentalist's wife "intimately," he said he hoped to "get laid" later that evening, and he said he "dropped five thousand dollars" on a lap dancer. Plus, he repeatedly dropped the semantic "F bomb" in conversation and from the stage. To the credit of the mentalist community, I noticed no epidemic interest in his brand of "theism"!

My Identity and Role with the Mentalists

Let me report on who I am with the people in magic and mentalism. The mentalist subculture deplores nonperforming "lurkers" who only want access to the art's secrets. They also resent "evangelists," who sometimes inhabit their conferences and Internet discussions to promote *any* religious, political, or philosophical cause or point of view—including atheism!

I am primarily involved in their fellowship as a fellow mentalist—enjoying the company in which we stimulate each other, encourage each other, give each other feedback, and learn from each other. I got into magic as a boy six years before I became a confessing Christian. I got into it once again a year before I discovered its connection to my vocation.

Vocationally, I have a long-standing interest in secularity, with a long-term focus on Christianity's ministry to people in secular Western societies. I was a convert out of secularity, as a teenager in Miami, Florida; my mom and dad became Christians after I did. While in divinity school, I spent a summer with the people at Muscle Beach who were even more secular than I had been. I did a PhD in communication studies at Northwestern, to gain perspective on the communication of Christianity's vision and message to secular populations with little or no Christian memory. I interviewed secular people, I interviewed converts out of secularity, I studied a number of Christian communicators to secular people, I studied churches who reach people with no church to transfer from, and I studied two great historical Christian movements to pre-Christian populations. I wrote several books from what I learned.[9]

9. See *How to Reach Secular People* (1992), *Church for the Unchurched* (1996), *The Celtic Way of Evangelism* (2000, 2010 rev. ed.), *Radical Outreach* (2003), *The Apostolic Congregation* (2009), *The Recovery of a Contagious Methodist Movement*

When I discovered how many magicians and mentalists are secular, and how many of them are skeptics, that discovery catalyzed greater interest in studying mentalism and becoming involved with its people. I could even sense the possible "hand of God" in my awakened interest in magic. Some Christians would expect that I would have entered the mentalist's society primarily as an evangelist; maybe I should have, but I have not, and have no plans to engage with this society in that way. One reason is that I studied the culture enough to discern that any overt "proselytizing" would be counterproductive.

My experiences with the muscle crowd and the mind readers may not be typical of what other Christians would find. For one thing, I am an ordained Methodist pastor. That is an important personal variable because, with about half of the unchurched population, you lose your credibility the day you get ordained! You are now perceived as a paid propagandist, or a membership recruiter, for the institutional church. (Herb Miller used to joke that, for this reason, faith sharing is the only "game" in which the "amateurs" outperform the "professionals," two to one![10])

In any case, my primary role with the mentalists is to be a mentalist! Within a couple of years, I had read the dozen or so books that any "serious" hobbyist-mentalist would know, and my knowledge of communication theory helped me to rather quickly become a "player" in their eyes. Very early (I think always), I identified myself as a Christian, or a theologian, or a writer for the church and the academy. In conversations, I am not only interested in the best mentalism book they have read this year, or their favorite approach to the Add-a-Number effect; I am interested in them as people.

At the annual mentalism convention, in Las Vegas, a conversation, question, or need surfaces two, three, or four times per day, almost always

---

(2011), and *Should We Change Our Game Plan?* (2013)—all published by Abingdon Press.

10.   Herb Miller told this joke at a workshop.

at their initiative, to which I respond out of faith's resources. Some of the conversations, sometimes including conversation with God, do not end at the convention but continue in e-mail conversations, in phone calls, or at the next year's convention. By now, several men have become Christians, and several more have "recovered" from lapsed discipleship and are active Christians once again. They would all report that conversation with George Hunter is one reason for their new, or renewed, life. I provided one or two links in the chain of experiences that helped them to believe and cross the line and commit. The people of their local church, and often one or more family members or friends, did most of the heavy lifting. "No one can say 'Jesus is Lord' except by the Holy Spirit" (1 Cor 12:3); all of us in apostolic ministry are junior partners.

In other cases, I have exercised a "ministry of presence." I have left a whole lot up to God and their families, friends, and local churches. But the "presence" role actually fits with my evolving understanding of how evangelism actually takes place with secular populations in the West. It begins by one or preferably a critical mass of Christians being present with and for them in their world, it continues through "the ministry of conversation"—not one-way, but two-way conversation, not one conversation but multiple conversations over time—and it continues as they become involved in a community of faith; after all, the faith is "more caught than taught." When they discover that they believe, we invite them to commit, and then we help them begin the life of a disciple.

Yet Another Appeal for Christian Presence

If it doesn't begin with our presence in their world, it doesn't usually begin at all. Christian disciples are called to be "the salt of the earth" and "the light of the world"; a disciple's assignment involves being in and for, but not of, the world, as "ambassadors for Christ."

Alas, as I have suggested, *that* is the supreme (if unacknowledged) problem for a growing number of professing Christians. Christianity teaches, and the world often experiences, that pre-Christian people who have not experienced reconciliation with God, who have not yet discovered God's purpose for their lives, and are not yet Jesus-followers, are "lost," like "sheep without a shepherd." Christianity teaches that lost people cannot, by themselves, find the life that they deeply want and were meant for. They search for life, but in all the wrong places. Lost people need to be found; if they are to be found, they are more likely to be found on their turf than in churches! Jesus, "the friend of sinners," calls his disciples to follow him in the world in compassionate presence and ministry.

That is a problem because most Christians are headed in the opposite direction. Christians are increasingly disengaging from "the world." The people in their friendship networks are increasingly Christians and decreasingly pagans; some church leaders do not know many (or any) non-Christian people; they may assume there aren't many. Christians are spending more time with Christians and less with pre-Christians, more time in their church and less in the community.

I could proliferate examples of The Great Abdication *ad nauseum*, but that is no longer necessary. No one now denies that this is happening; indeed, most Christians can give "reasons" for disengaging. I was conversing with an evangelical young father who was working a second job to afford private Christian schooling for his children. I said that a part of me wished that more caring articulate Christians like him were involved with the local public schools. He replied, "There are *reasons* why we don't want our children in the public schools."

Exactly. Christians are finding more and more reasons to disengage from the community. The cumulative effect of those decisions is the slow-but-steady emergence of Christian cultural enclaves. One day, if this trend continues, the Christian population will be as "ghettoized" as the Jewish people once were; this will be the unintended consequence of a great many choices.

With the trend into enclaves now established, the paradigm of the Christian life has shifted. Enclave Christianity is now widely assumed to be "normal" Christianity. When people like me (and other "mavericks") spend time visiting with people at the local gym, or a magic club, or an airport bar, or even at a local civic club, that is increasingly perceived as an "abnormal" thing for a Christian to do.

My exploration with the muscle crowd and the mind readers has reminded me of the next step in understanding the extensive mission field that secularization has produced in the West. Understanding what most secular people have in common, and profiling the general population much as Willow Creek Community Church once profiled "Unchurched Harry and Mary,"[11] is still useful in making sense of the cultural context for Christian mission in the West—useful but, often, not quite enough.

The next step is understanding, more specifically, each secular affinity group. There is no shortcut to understanding them, but the process can be streamlined. With a team of Christians (preferably), become involved with some affinity group with whom you share their interest. Spend time with them, and converse with them, especially with the best informants you can find. Read what they read, do what is necessary to win credibility. Record your data and your insights, and reflect until patterns, a profile, and points of contact become obvious.

11. See *How to Reach Secular People,* 156–67.

We have known, at least since St. Patrick's evangelization of the Irish, that the Christian movement typically advances *as* we understand the people. The more we understand a target population, the more we will know what to say and what to do in ministry. The less we understand them, the more disconnected, clueless, and useless to them we will be.

Chapter Five

Serving and Reaching "Affinity Groups"

T he first two chapters reflected from the four Gospels' accounts of the earliest Christian movement and proposed that Christianity's mission, locally and globally, is its main business (or should be.) We said that a "real church" is an "ecclesia"—the "called out" people of God whom the Lord shapes into an "apostolate," the "sent out" people of God. The first four chapters featured the public presence that is a prerequisite to effective mission, everywhere. This chapter features Christianity's mission as an outreach to all people, in their many families, clans, tribes, classes, peer groups, peoples, and other affinity groups.

The earliest Christian mission perceived and engaged the earth's fascinating demographic complexity in ways that today's church leaders are still struggling to rediscover. I am not competent to nuance all of the relevant texts in scripture. (The only Hebrew terms I can even remember are Elohim and Taj Mahal!) But the following thoughts are basic.[1]

---

1. I found Terrence L Donaldson's article "Nations" in volume four (231–38) of *The New Interpreters Dictionary of the Bible* (Nashville: Abingdon Press, 2009) to be very useful in sorting this out.

The God of Abraham formed Abraham's descendants into a "nation" and gave them a distinctive role in a world teeming with "nations"—in the sense of "peoples." In that era, a distinctive nation occupied a more-or-less specific territory (but some "nations" were nomadic) and had a king and an army; a distinctive culture, religious worldview, language, or dialect; and they had a name. Exodus 3, for example, forecasts Israel to a land in proximity to the Canaanites, the Hittites, the Amorites, the Perizzites, the Hivites, and the Jebusites. Many other peoples populated that ancient Mediterranean world. Isaiah (49:6) tells us that Israel's assignment among the peoples was to serve as a "light to the nations."

By the New Testament period, the demographics paradigm had shifted. Some "nations" had scattered and were less identified with a territory. Under Roman rule, many nations no longer had a king or an army. The focus shifted toward what we now call "ethnicity"; a people were known by features like their name, language, customs, and religious views and practices. The term *nation* never meant the same thing as the modern "nation state"—which was a later invention of the eighteenth-century European Enlightenment. Furthermore, by the New Testament period the demographic awareness extended to other sorts of human groups—like Samaritans, Zealots, Sadducees, lepers, and many others—who had something in common, experienced affinity, conversed with one another, and influenced each other's choices, lives, and view of reality.

Jesus, in Matthew 28, commissioned his movement to make disciples among *panta ta ethne*. After the earliest Christian movement reached Gentiles in Antioch, the movement adapted to, and engaged, an incredibly wide range of clans, tribes, and other people groups in their language and on their turf; the movement adapted to each tongue and culture and was often contagious. This demographic strategy for reaching the peoples lasted for more than a century.

The Roman Empire, however, expected the realm's many peoples to speak Latin, to become culturally Roman, and to conform in other ways. In time, the now "established" Church of the empire prescribed one expression of Christianity for everyone. The "peoples" perspective was largely lost; from time to time, however, leaders like St. Martin of Tours, St. Patrick, and John Wesley regained it and launched new Christian movements.

Donald McGavran's Rediscovery

In the 1950s, a missionary scholar named Donald McGavran experienced another rediscovery of the principle, although much of the Western church—in the wake of the civil rights struggle, was not quite ready.[2] After years of field research and reflection, McGavran began commending (what came to be known as) the "Church Growth" approach to understanding and informing effective mission and evangelism. His speaking and writing about how churches reach people groups, historically and worldwide, triggered questions, charges, criticisms, and an occasional "hornets' nest," especially when he explained that the faith spreads with less effort and more contagion within "homogeneous" population units.

In his studies of growing churches, McGavran never set out to discover this principle. (Honest field researchers do not always find what they expect to find or hope to find! Indeed, when a researcher's "discoveries" always ratify his or her prior views, the "research" becomes suspect.) Furthermore, McGavran never regarded his "homogeneous Unit" (HU) principle as his most important insight, but it received more constant static than all of his other themes combined—at least

---

2. For McGavran's full story, and enduring significance, see Gary L. McIntosh, *Donald McGavran: A Biography of the Twentieth Century's Premier Missiologist* (Church Leader Insights USA, 2015).

until the early twenty-first century.[3] Samuel Escobar's charges in the mid-1970s, that the principle accommodates "to the sinfulness of society" and that church growth people are attempting "to perpetuate segregation for the sake of numerical growth,"[4] were repeated for an entire generation; it became a "politically correct" mantra among thousands of church leaders.

McGavran's most concise (and most quoted) version of the theory stated, **"People like to become Christians without crossing racial, linguistic, or class barriers."**[5] He later regretted that the statement had only implied the most important adjective: **"culture"** barriers. This was an unfortunate omission because culture barriers are formidable—in part because they are invisible barriers that reside subconsciously within people, and in part because culture barriers pervade (and hide within) the other barriers.

McGavran also reflected that "ethnic" barriers would have communicated his meaning more clearly than "racial" barriers. Many American Christian leaders, who had experienced the civil rights movement, saw his statement as an excuse (or even a rationale) for segregation. Since McGavran was raised in India and spent most of his career in India, he was not influenced directly by the United States's civil rights struggle.

---

3. The "homogeneous unit" issue was virtually ignored by the five writers in *Evaluating the Church Growth Movement* (Gary McIntosh, ed. Zondervan, 2004); the term does not even warrant inclusion in the book's fifteen-page index. This is (presumably) because, for serious readers of church growth literature, the issue was sufficiently settled by such comprehensive and nuanced interpretations as Peter Wagner's doctoral dissertation at the University of Southern California, later published as *Our Kind of People: The Ethical Dimension of Church Growth in America* (Louisville: John Knox Press, 1979). People who do not follow the literature, however, may still express discomfort when they encounter the term.

4. Samuel Escobar, "Evangelism and Man's Search for Freedom, Justice, and Fulfillment," in J. D. Douglas, ed., *Let the Earth Hear His Voice* (Minneapolis: World Wide Publications, 1975), 323.

5. Donald A. McGavran, revised by C. Peter Wagner, *Understanding Church Growth*, 3rd ed. (Grand Rapids, MI: William B. Eerdmans, 1990), 163.

Many American church leaders were puzzled by McGavran's usual response to the "segregation" charge. He explained that the HU principle was not intended to serve as "a principle for excluding anyone, but for including everyone, because God wants no one left out."[6] He believed that we should take the principle's inclusionary power seriously, because it has enabled the great "People Movements" of Christianity's past and present. In most movements into the Christian faith, many people of a tribe (or some other social unit) become Christians through an expanding web of interpersonal influences. McGavran named these webs "the bridges of God." He observed, "The Christian faith flows well within each piece of the mosaic, but tends to stop at linguistic and ethnic barriers."[7]

McGavran reached the early insights behind the principle during his lengthy career as a mission teacher, executive, and church planter in India—with its entrenched caste system. He consistently observed that, when you invited seekers or new Christians of one caste to join a church composed principally of people from another caste, they usually resisted. (McGavran was beginning to discover that the barriers preventing people from following Christ are usually "more social than theological.") Furthermore, he observed that when

---

6. McGavran also affirmed the integrity of *ethnic identity*, and the value of *diversity* within a society. He observed that multicultural churches often manifest an (unintentional) homogenizing effect—in which some of the peoples "melt" into the majority culture and lose some (or much) of their ethnic identity. Indigenous homogeneous churches help preserve each people's language, culture, and identity. So, he suggested, "One goal of missions is to multiply churches in every homogeneous unit, culturally in harmony with that unit, jealously guarding its cultural diversity, and considering the tribe or caste, the clan or other unit of God's order of preservation, to be respected till God replaces it." Donald A. McGavran, "The Genesis and Strategy of the Homogeneous Unit Principle." Unpublished paper presented at the Consultation on the Homogeneous Unit Principle, sponsored by the Lausanne Theology and Education Group, at Fuller Theological Seminary, Pasadena, CA, May 31–June 2, 1977.

7. Donald A. McGavran, "The Dimensions of World Evangelization," in *Let the Earth Hear His Voice*, J. D. Douglas, ed. (Minneapolis: World Wide Publications, 1975), 100.

someone from one caste did join a church of people predominately from another caste, their families and kindred perceived their decision as abandonment, or even traitorous; such converts could be shunned, isolated, or declared "dead."

McGavran became convinced that the price of "social dislocation" that Indian converts typically paid for becoming Christians is not required by the gospel, and that the perceived requirement to "leave your people and join another people" to become a Christian was a "false stumbling block" to becoming Christian. He believed that one principle of Christianity in mission, therefore, should be to remove this and all other identifiable false stumbling blocks, so that people could better consider the one true stumbling block of "Jesus Christ and him crucified." For McGavran, this insight demanded a strategy to plant churches in any population unit in which cultural norms were stacked against their people ever "joining another people."

As Donald McGavran came to study churches and peoples far beyond India and its unique caste system—from West Africa and East Asia to Latin America and Oceania, he observed similar social barriers but on different lines. The people in one tribe usually resisted joining a church of another tribe; or the people of one class resisted joining a church of another class; or most of an expatriate population resisted becoming involved in a church of nationals.

Choosing and Defining a Term

McGavran found no term that adequately referred to the entire range of social groups who are much more likely to respond to Christianity when commended by "our kind of people." So he invented the term *homogeneous unit*. Like many "first draft" terms in the historical development of academic fields (*Symbolic Interactionism* is another that comes to mind), this one "stuck" longer than it should have. Since the term's referent was more intuitively understood at first, McGavran and his protégés revised its definition over time.

Essentially, the term refers to **any group of people with some characteristic in common who, because of that characteristic, tend to a) identify with each other, b) trust each other, c) communicate more naturally than with people outside the group, and d) influence each other's choices, lives, and worldview.** So, by this, perspective, most Meru people in Nairobi, Gypsy people in Bucharest, Haitian people in Miami, Appalachian tire factory workers in Akron, counterculture young adults in London, deaf people in Chicago, and drug addicts in Hong Kong are homogeneous units. People of certain vocations, subcultures, and interest groups in a specific city, such as medical people, educators, artists, bodybuilders, taxi drivers, or golfers, might or might not function as a homogeneous unit. You would have to interview them to find out; while taxi drivers in Seoul are a homogeneous group, those in Chicago are not. Tall people, people with red hair, Purdue graduates, and Buick drivers are probably not homogeneous units anywhere; while they have a characteristic in common, they do not especially identify with each other, or trust each other, or communicate more naturally, or influence each other's lives.

Within many population units, however, one can observe a range of responses to pluralism. So in some homogeneous populations, some group members resist involvement with a church of another people, but other members are open. In heterogeneous societies, some ethnic groups "melt" and become "assimilated" with the majority population more rapidly than other ethnic groups.[8] The receptivity of other ethnic groups to a "conglomerate church" option might be greater now than before, or later than now.

---

8. See Tetsunao Yamamori, "How to Reach Ethnics," in Win Arn, ed., *The Pastor's Church Growth Handbook* (The Institute for American Church Growth, 1979), 171–84.

McGavran observed some situations in which there was little or no resistance to joining a heterogeneous church, but some outcomes were nevertheless undesirable. In Peru or Bolivia, for instance, you could often persuade Aymara Indians to join a church with a majority Quechua membership. In such "conglomerate" churches, however, the leaders were nearly always Quechuas; Quechuas had dominated Aymaras for so long that both peoples assumed that Quechua leadership was nature's arrangement. (And Aymaras and Quechuas both deferred to Mestizos.) So, if you believed that God wanted to develop and empower Aymara Christian leaders, for an Aymara Christian movement, this seemed to require some churches that are essentially (but not exclusively) Aymara churches.

McGavran observed that culturally conglomerate churches are, indeed, a desirable and socially possible option for many peoples, especially in cities. He believed that we are called to plant and build churches of many peoples wherever that is possible and, in the contexts where we do not know what is possible for whom, we should offer receptive peoples both conglomerate church and homogeneous church options. McGavran regarded a homogeneous unit church as a penultimate form of the church, and he preferred conglomerate churches, but **his controlling issue was not what kind of church would be best for Christians to worship in, but what kind of church could reach a pre-Christian population.**[9] Often, you will reach many more of them through a church that is essentially of, by, and for their people, because most seekers are attracted to a church where they identify with the people, feel that they are understood, and perceive that Christianity is for "people like us."

Indeed, even when you can reach new people through a conglomerate church of multiple homogeneous units, you have to take each population seriously, and you offer ministries that are indigenous

9.   I have emphasized this statement, because most of the HU principle's critics have missed this point *in toto*.

to their culture and relevant to their needs. So, for example, the leaders of a conglomerate church that effectively reaches (say) Anglo professional people, first-generation Mexican-Americans, first-generation Filipino-Americans, mentally handicapped people, deaf people, and addictive people will understand each population, and some of their ministries, groups, and congregations are focused for them.

Renaming, and Refining, the Principle

People who work in the behavioral sciences know that McGavran's principle is neither extraordinary nor astonishing. Leaders in several fields have, independently, reached similar insights. Political reform leaders, for instance, have been known to achieve their objectives by identifying, engaging, training, and mobilizing "affinity groups." Intercultural communicators and change agents have learned to work for their objectives through the natural "reference groups" in which people bond, and find identity, and interpret messages from the wider world.

Scholars in the dozen fields who research the "Diffusion of Innovations" have learned to take communication micro-channels very seriously. So, Everett Rogers writes, "An obvious principle of human communication is that the transfer of ideas occurs most frequently between two individuals who are similar, or homophilous.... More effective communication occurs when two or more individuals...share common meanings and a mutual subcultural language, and are alike in personal and social characteristics."[10] Scholars in several other fields make routine use of (some version of) the HU concept, by whatever name.

---

10. Everett M. Rogers, *Diffusion of Innovations*, 5th ed. (New York: The Free Press, 2003), 19.

I now prefer the terms *affinity groups* and *people units* as the best available terms that communicate the most generally, with the least baggage. Nevertheless, people without an interdisciplinary education should be able to move past any initial discomfort by reflecting on the social communication barriers we face in Christian mission, one at a time.

Language Barriers

No one with cross-cultural mission experience ever disputes the daunting reality of language barriers. Anyone, for instance, who has ever attempted to employ several languages in one service, or has even attempted to translate (say) an English language service into several other tongues, concurrently or sequentially, has experienced the near impossibility of the task, and the enormous tradeoffs involved. Indeed, among people with cross-cultural experience, the case for affinity group churches based on languages is obvious.

Church leaders without cross-cultural experience, however, often demonstrate "linguistic blindness"; their own language seems so perfectly natural to them that they are naïve about language barriers and the complex challenge of overcoming "Babel." For example, I spoke for Wheaton College's annual debate series in 2003. The topic had to do with "seeker churches." (I spoke on the team affirming the seeker church model.) One of the two speakers on the other team was senior pastor of a downtown mainline church in San Diego. He charged that seeker churches are "exclusive" because they "target" specific groups of people and they even "market" the church to "appeal" to such people; he preferred churches like his that, he reported, is "an inclusive church for everyone in San Diego."

The previous week, I had telephoned the ESL department of San Diego's school system—asking, "In your school system, how many languages do your children speak in their homes?" The staff person replied, "About 115." In the debate's cross-examination period, I asked the pastor, "In how many languages is your church doing ministry, besides English?" He replied that their entire ministry, currently, was in English. I then suggested that if a church is doing ministry in only one of the 115 languages of its city, it might not actually be experienced as an "inclusive church" by every linguistic population in the city!

Okay, I now regret that exchange, in which I embarrassed a committed pastor who had led a downtown church to stay downtown and find some ways to be faithful there. That church's linguistic blindness, however, is widely entrenched in American Protestant Christianity. In the most multilingual industrial or post-industrial nation on earth (in which one in five inhabitants speaks and dreams in a first language other than English, and in a nation in which the citizens of almost every city speak thirty languages or more), most of our churches navigate their life in local mission by the assumption that English is the best language for reaching and serving everyone in the city. Most American Protestant leaders are as entrenched in the assumption that English is best for everyone as the Roman Catholic Church, for seventeen centuries prior to Vatican II, ever assumed that Latin was best for everyone.

North American Anglos, however, have no monopoly on linguistic blindness; in many nations, the dominant linguistic population regards their own language as "normal," and they assume that other populations will become bilingual (or will even abandon their original language!) and "worship with us." For example, anthropologist Steve Ybarrola informs me that the leaders of Spain's Protestant churches relate to Spain's one and a half million Basque people from a similar policy: Basque people should worship in Spanish, in Spaniard churches. Most of Spain's Basque people can function in Spanish, but it is not the heart language of many Basques.

Spain's Roman Catholic churches, since the Vatican II departure from the "Latin for everyone" policy, now feature many Basque masses and, though the secularization of Europe has not bypassed

Spain, visitors in Spain now meet Basque Catholics in fair numbers. No Protestant churches, however, feature Basque language services or congregations; consequently, there are few Basque Protestants—although some now meet, on their own initiative, in Basque language Bible studies or informal fellowships.

McGavran's well-known statement told us, in part, "People like to become Christians without crossing...linguistic...barriers." The time is already past for church leaders in many nations to welcome that blinding flash of the obvious. How can we justify continuing what many peoples experience as linguistic racism?

Culture Barriers

Cultural barriers were clearly implied in McGavran's statement; that was the type of barrier he spoke about most often. Anthropologist Geert Hofstede characterizes culture as "the software of the mind," meaning our culture is the pattern of learned and shared assumptions, beliefs, attitudes, values, and customs that our socialization "programmed" into our consciousness.[11] Because of their different socialization experiences, two peoples will see the world (at least somewhat) differently. A generation before Hofstede, E. T. Hall characterized culture as "the silent language."[12] A culture, Hall taught us, has nine other "primary message systems" in addition to its language. Messages communicated through our language engage us (or miss us) quite consciously, but messages communicated through our other message systems engage us (or miss us) subconsciously.

Many missionaries experienced these realities long before the anthropologists gave us a vocabulary to reflect about them. The Christian world mission has often known that, to reach a people, you have to communicate in their language and, in many other ways, do

---

11. See Geert Hofstede, *Culture's Consequences* (New York: SAGE Publications, Inc; 1984).

12. Edward T. Hall, *The Silent Language* (New York: Fawcett World Library, 1959).

ministry in ways that are indigenous to their culture. An indigenous church has its limitations, however; indigenous Christianity tends to produce and grow homogeneous churches, for no more profound reason than (say) a genre of music that engages the people of one culture will fail to engage (or may even "turn off") the people of another culture. In New York City, for example, the jazz congregation of Redeemer Presbyterian Church reaches people who like jazz more effectively than people who dislike jazz!

So, indigenous Christianity tends, de facto, to exclude people for whom the church's style, language, aesthetics, and music are not culturally relevant to them. This is not exclusion by design; anyone is welcome, and leaders can be ecstatic when a congregation reaches people it does not target. But, McGavran believed that indigenous Christianity is inclusion by design. McGavran saw the world as a beautiful "mosaic" of many different cultures. The church's great mandate is to plant indigenous churches, and thereby make disciples, in every "piece" of the mosaic, and thereby include every people group in the Christian movement.

Class Barriers

Eugene Nida taught that every society has about six (vertically scaled) socio-economic "classes" of people—based on factors like ancestry, wealth, education, talent, and leadership.[13] (In a marvelous stroke of academic clarity, Nida named them the upper-upper, lower-upper, upper-middle, lower-middle, upper-lower, and lower-lower classes!) Very often, a given church will be most effective with one of those six classes, marginally effective with adjacent classes, and ineffective with more different classes. In the United States, historically, Episcopalians have engaged a different slice of humanity

---

13. See Eugene A. Nida, *Message and Mission: The Communication of the Christian Faith*, revised edition (Pasadena, CA; William Carey Library, 1990) especially chapter 10.

than Baptists. More specifically, we seldom find a church whose literate educated leaders are reaching preliterate people in any significant numbers. Baptists do not typically invite nonliterate people to group Bible studies and, understandably, nonliterate invitees would not likely accept an invitation. Moreover, for identical reasons, Episcopal churches do not often invite people who are unable to navigate the Book of Common Prayer.

We see the subtle power of class barriers when we observe that, in most of the well-known multiethnic churches that are popularly thought to be "heterogeneous," most of the attendees are from the same socio-economic class.[14] Since class barriers are usually experienced more from "the underside" (that is, we are more comfortable with them than they are with us), McGavran served the church by identifying class barriers as real, and by advocating new church planting for classes of people that the sponsoring church would like to reach but cannot.

Ethnic Barriers

McGavran also identified racial barriers among the types of barriers that people were reluctant to cross to become Christians. I cannot glibly dismiss that factor. When I became a Christian, at age seventeen, in the Fulford Methodist church in Miami, Florida, I might not have responded if the only Christians I met were Haitians who (I would have assumed) could not understand my "issues," with whom I (thought) I could not identify. In the years after I became a Christian, my capacity to identify with, and enjoy, other peoples expanded exponentially. Fourteen years after my conversion, I found

---

14.   For instance, the best-known multiethnic church in Lexington, Kentucky, is known as International Christian Fellowship. It meets in an auditorium in the University of Kentucky's Nursing School. At first blush, it looks astonishingly multiethnic, and it is; but the attendees are virtually all (a) young adults, (b) students or graduate students at UK, who have (c) all mastered English sufficiently to study for degrees in English—all of which makes ICF a pretty homogeneous congregation!

myself a pastor of a Methodist church of West Indies immigrant people in Birmingham, England. That was my most interesting and fulfilling period as a pastor, but fourteen years earlier that church probably could not have reached me, and probably would not have tried.

McGavran's field-analytic powers, however, really focused much more on "ethnic" barriers than "racial" barriers. McGavran's paradigm saw the world as essentially a "beautiful mosaic" of thousands of distinct ethno-linguistic peoples[15] as well as tens of thousands of other groups whose affinity with each other is based on some shared condition (such as poverty, or AIDS) or some shared experience (such as common education, or occupation). We must not deny, however, that "race" per se can be a barrier in major societies as scattered as the United States and South Africa. While I agree with McGavran that, to reach many peoples in many places we have to plant indigenous ethnic churches, I (more reluctantly) agree that, for some people in some places, we still have to plant churches that are essentially homogeneous, racially, to make initial discipleship possible for people of that race.

I also agree with McGavran's (deep but less known) conviction that, as we fulfill the Great Commission by teaching new disciples "to obey" all that Christ has commanded, this especially mandates us to help people discover much wider horizontal loves and loyalties, especially across ethnic barriers that still separate peoples from each other. This often happens spontaneously, though gradually. Lamin Sanneh reflects upon the history of evangelization in sub-Sahara Africa, where Christian movements typically began in many specific tribes. The early movement ministered and planted churches in each tribe, trained indigenous pastors, translated the scriptures into

---

15. McGavran's long-time colleague, anthropologist and historian Ralph Winter, proposed that there are approximately thirty thousand known distinct societies across the earth.

each tongue, and, in some cases, raised up hundreds of indigenous congregations, each worshiping in one of a dozen or more languages within a nation. In the process, the younger churches discovered the shared meanings and power that made them sisters and brothers in Christ. Many of Africa's thriving denominations today are multitribal and multilingual movements.[16]

These barriers often take different shapes in the West, where the barriers to faith are much less about race than some think, and rooted more in language, culture, and class differences. This can become most obvious when such differences are experienced within a race. Consider several examples from South Florida.

In Greater Miami, I observed several Cuban-American churches that were not engaging Mexicans or Latinos, nor the younger, more recent, blue-collar immigrants from Cuba. I observed several African-American churches that were not engaging recent West African expatriates. I observed several middle-class Anglo churches that were not engaging jet setters, dog-racing people, or trailer-park residents.

I also observed several cases in which the members of African American churches had gained education, prospered, and moved out to "better housing," while still driving back to their old neighborhood church. A lower socio-economic class of African Americans moved into the neighborhood. The church leaders did not understand their new neighbors, nor did they know where to begin in outreach; the new residents said the church "does not speak our language."

In each case, the barrier was not racial but related to culture, class, or ethnicity.

Sometimes, church leaders perceive the real barriers immediately. When (black) Haitian immigrants began flooding into South Florida, African American congregations quickly perceived the linguistic,

16. See Lamin Sanneh, *Translating the Message: The Missionary Impact on Culture* (Maryknoll, NY: Orbis, 1989).

culture, and class barriers and supported, from the beginning, the planting of Haitian churches.

Once we learn to "exegete" the differences between peoples, we will discover that the barriers are often less about race than we thought and more about ethnicity, class, and language, and much more about culture, than we thought.

Why This Really Matters

We can now nuance McGavran's cogent statement with more precision: **Churches find it more possible to reach pre-Christian people without requiring them to cross linguistic, cultural, ethnic, or class barriers to become new disciples.**[17]

I have listed, above, these barriers in order of their "height," or the difficulty for most people to cross them. **Linguistic barriers are usually the most formidable, cultural and ethnic barriers less so, and class barriers least so.** In some places, however, the latter two barriers can be more formidable than in other places. If two ethnic tribes have a history of warfare between them, for instance, the ethnic barrier may be higher. And some major societies still experience considerable class barriers, such as England and (especially) India. Furthermore, we can conjecture that more people can cross one of the four barriers than two, more can cross two than three, and so on. **Without any of these barriers, outreach to most people is still an apostolic challenge; so in most contexts it is useful to remove as many "false stumbling blocks" as possible.**

17. C. Peter Wagner once essentialized such factors in his "Ethclass" model of the homogeneous unit. Building upon the work of Milton Gordon in ethnicity and assimilation theory, Wagner contended that a homogeneous unit, at least in the United States, is usually a "sub-society created by the intersection of the vertical stratifications of ethnicity with the horizontal stratification of social class." *Our Kind of People*, 61–62.

Perceiving Mission Fields Through a "People Unit" Lens

As churches consider their strategy for outreach ministry, they discover that seeing people as belonging to "people units" is much more effective than seeing them in "political units." This is true at every level, but examples at two levels should make it clear.

In the late nineteenth century, American Presbyterian missionaries served people and planted churches in Guatemala. By the mid-twentieth century, the Presbyterian Church of Guatemala was self-governing and self-supporting, and so the missionaries returned home. To some degree, however, the new church's name was a myth. Guatemala is a nation-state of twenty-four different language populations; the church that the missionaries left behind was essentially a church of **one** of those twenty-four peoples. Logically, instead of coming home, the missionaries should have moved across a mountain range to engage another of the twenty-four peoples.

However, the Guatemalan Presbyterian leaders saw their land as a field of many language peoples. They gained some new American allies and engaged in cross-cultural ministry with several other language populations. Today, the church is no longer "national" in name only.

In many nations across the earth, a denomination may carry the nation's name but has essentially reached only one of the nation's peoples. The Methodist Church of Kenya is another example. Once planted by British Methodism, autonomous since 1967, now numbering over 1,000 churches and over 450,000 members, it is still essentially a Meru church. It matters whether you define your mission field in political units or people units.

Or consider the local Methodist church in the small town of Possum, Oklahoma,[18] where I once spent some time. In a town of almost two thousand people, the church's average attendance was about fifty—down from about seventy twenty years before. With that attendance, the church was the second largest of the six chapels in the town or on its outskirts. At least 70 percent of Possum, Oklahoma, people were unchurched. I engaged in several days of door-to-door visitation with unchurched people. They never once referred to the Methodist church by its denominational name; they referred to "the Williams church."

I spent some time with the church's membership records. Sure enough, almost every person who had ever joined the church was related to "Old Man Williams" (by now deceased) by blood or marriage. Eight names on the membership roll seemed to be exceptions, but there was no record or memory that they had taught Sunday school, or sang in the choir, or served on the board; the several still alive were all inactive.

The "Williams church" was a prototypical, stereotypical "clan-bound" church. Many thousands of them dot the United States landscape, although some include several friends and their families—more similar to the "household" churches reflected in the New Testament. The clan-based church is one natural form that churches take in many places. In such places, we often need more of them!

Most of the people I interviewed door-to-door reported that they liked the Williams people but had no interest in joining "their" church. When I started asking if they'd be interested in starting a new church in town, almost half expressed interest. When I reported this possibility to the regional Methodist superintendent, with names

18. This is based on an actual case, but that does not really matter. One finds a great many thousands of small, clan-bound open-country and small-town congregations across the United States. To avoid embarrassing anyone, I have changed the name of the town and the surname popularly connected to the church.

and addresses, he replied, "One Methodist church in a town that size is plenty!" Looking back, I am sure he saw all of the town's people as citizens within the same political unit. If he had perceived them in people units, he might have responded differently.

Outreach to Target "Affinity Groups"

By now, many churches have discovered that they have to "target" a distinct under-served population to have a chance to reach them; they may experience this as a regretful necessity, but also as an opportunity. Furthermore, when they target one group, virtually always they are not intending to exclude anyone. Anyone is welcomed. My experiences in visiting churches have always confirmed this. When I visited a Swahili Roman Catholic congregation in Nairobi, no one cared that I was Anglo, no one checked to see if I was Catholic, no one tested my Swahili competence. When I visited a deaf Baptist congregation in Bucharest, no doorkeeper inquired whether I was deaf, or understood Romanian, or the sign language, or even whether I was Baptist! When I visited a recovery congregation at a Vineyard church in Cincinnati, no one checked at the door to see whether I was an addict or in recovery; but, following the benediction, several people befriended me, just in case. The invisible social barriers that often restrain people groups from joining particular churches are usually more externally than internally experienced; the church wants them, but "they" feel they cannot connect.

Since the purpose of an affinity unit congregation is to reach people the church cannot otherwise reach, I do run across very occasional projects that are (reluctantly) exclusive. For instance, some meetings of recovery congregations are "closed" to nonaddictive people; this exclusion encourages addicts to share at these meetings, who would never share in the presence of people who "just wouldn't understand."

Again, Springs of Living Water Church (springschurch.org) in Winnipeg, Manitoba, has eight worshipping congregations that meet at five locations across the city, including an inner-city campus. Their Saturday evening congregation targets young adults eighteen to thirty. They check IDs! They do not like to exclude anyone, but they discovered that they have to make that congregation exclusively for that age cohort population, in that city, to reach many of Winnipeg's pre-Christian young adults. The church's leaders assured me that this policy is a "controlled exception"; they provide many other experiences to fulfill the church's motto—"One Church, One Family, Many Locations."

Once upon a Time, in Scotland

Dr. Andrew Walls once spent a week with our graduate students and faculty at Asbury Theological Seminary's School of World Mission and Evangelism. Andrew Walls is arguably the greatest living historian of Christian mission, the greatest since Kenneth Scott Latourette. One day, Walls referred to the fact that he is a Scottish Methodist. It occurred to me that I had never met one before, and I recalled that, while eighteenth-century Methodism had been a movement in England, Wales, and even parts of Ireland, it never "took off" in Scotland. I asked Walls why. He recounted the following history.

The first people in Scotland to respond to Wesley and his apostolic band were fishermen and their families, mainly (as I recall) along Scotland's east coast. Within one generation, there were Methodist chapels and societies in many fishing villages. Fishermen and their families, however, were endogamous, and in other ways kept to themselves and were isolated from other vocational clans in Scotland. Methodism in Scotland became socially perceived as the church for fishermen. Few other Scots were interested in (or being perceived as) leaving their people and joining the fishermen! I later found out that a much smaller Methodist movement once broke out in some mining villages, but miners and their families were also endogamous. So, essentially, Methodism in Scotland became a small sealed-off movement among those two people groups. Today Methodism is small in Scotland, and, I am told, almost every Scots Methodist is a descendant of those fishing and mining converts.

So we keep rediscovering the "homogeneous unit" principle whether we want to or not! We celebrate heterogeneous churches whenever we find them, and we yearn and work for more of them. We are called to offer conglomerate congregations to all people who will respond to their appeal, and we need many more such congregations. As I suggested, however, many conglomerate churches are, all criteria considered, more homogeneous than we once thought.

We have also discovered that many "homogeneous churches" are more heterogeneous than we thought. In any city, several types of congregations usually demonstrate this: granting the one characteristic they have in common, many recovery congregations, or deaf congregations, or peace congregations, or ethnic minority language congregations often reach people from a much wider range of cultures and/or classes than almost any other church in the city.

I'd be willing to wager that most of those Methodist "fishermen's churches" in Scotland's coastal villages were involving people from a wider range of classes (like fishermen with a fleet of boats, and fishermen with one boat, and fishermen who worked for the others) than was the nearby congregation of "The Church of Scotland"— that defined itself as the National Church for everyone!

Chapter Six

One More Time: What Is Our Main Business?

T he first chapter featured Peter Drucker's essential first question for leaders of all organizations, including churches: "What is our main business?" Folks are fond of the line, "The main thing is to make the main thing the main thing." Okay, but it begs the bigger question: What is "the main thing"?

The first two chapters drew from the four Gospels (especially Luke) and proposed that Christianity's main business is its **mission** to pre-Christian people and people groups, locally and globally. As Jesus called, and later sent, his first disciples, so a "real church" begins as an "ecclesia"—the "called out" people of God whom the Lord shapes into an "apostolate," the "sent out" people of God. The mission of the one, holy, catholic, and apostolic movement is an outreach ministry to, and in behalf of, the community and the world. That was the earliest Christian movement's main business, and many later Christian movements (such as Protestant denominations and Roman Catholic "orders") had similar launches.

We saw that, as the early Christian movement became more of an institution, a generation's church leaders often changed their minds about Christianity's main business. A generic historical sketch explains (more or less) how this happened, repeatedly: A young Christian movement reaches and serves new people and multiplies churches that engage more new people, and so on. In time, the movement develops an organization to train priests or pastors, print music and literature, and to support the churches in many ways.

Eventually, however, the organization becomes an end in itself. The organization soon devolves into an institution. The institution has all but forgotten or, more often, has "improved" upon the younger movement's main business; the current leaders, often with industrial-strength hubris, assume they know better than the movement's founders. By now, the main business of most of the local churches is to support (and conform to) the institution and its revised agenda. In time, the churches internalize the wider institution's self-serving and self-preserving agenda.

Considering "Church Health" and "Church Growth"

The first chapter suggested that church leaders have often redefined their main business in one or more of (at least) ten ways. In recent history, one of those ten ways—the quest to achieve a church's greater "health" (or "revival," or "renewal," or "revitalization," or "vibrancy") has become the near-entrenched consensus in the minds of a great many church leaders.

The main business of many Western churches has become the attainment of "church health." In the late twentieth century, a research and training team led by Christian Schwarz, son of a (Lutheran) German state church pastor, rode this wave and focused this widespread interest. The team developed a questionnaire and surveyed over one thousand churches, in eighteen languages, in thirty-two countries, over a ten-year period. They reflected on their data and then staked out a distinctive claim: church growth necessarily follows from "church health"—as defined by eight characteristics.

Schwarz then published Natural Church Development: A Guide to Eight Essential Qualities of Healthy Churches.[1] Many church leaders across Europe loved it (in part because it was not an American export!). Within ten years, more than thirty language editions were published. In the United States, Conservative Baptist executive David Wetzler read the book; he believed in it so much that he mortgaged his home to fund its English translation and publication. Wetzler's ChurchSmart Resources published the book in 1996; it quickly sold more than 100,000 copies in North America alone. Natural Church Development's website (www.ncd-international .org) now reports partner leaders, churches, and organizations in over sixty countries.

Based on survey data from thirty core members in the surveyed churches, Schwarz claims that when churches focus on attaining eight known qualities of healthy churches, the churches should experience those very qualities in greater measure (and should grow as a result). Stressing the importance of the adjectives (more than the nouns), Natural Church Development (NCD) features these church health qualities:

1. Empowering Leadership

2. Gift-Oriented Ministry

3. Passionate Spirituality

4. Functional Structures

5. Inspiring Worship

6. Holistic Small Groups

---

1. Christian A. Schwarz, *Natural Church Development: A Guide to Eight Essential Qualities of Healthy Churches* (Carol Stream, IL: ChurchSmart Resources, 1996).

7. Need-Oriented Evangelism

8. Loving Relationships[2]

NCD works with churches that want greater health (and growth). The NCD website reports that the organization now has data from tens of thousands of churches on six continents. NCD claims that 85 percent of the churches they have trained have experienced subsequent growth.[3] Their website assures us, "This emphasis on church health has proven to be the key to ongoing growth and multiplication."

In the United States, the spread of interest in NCD was remarkably uneven. After a ten-year presence in the USA, it registered no blip on many radar screens. Schwarz's book had not been reviewed in the *Journal for the Scientific Study of Religion or the Review of Religious Research.* The world's leading sociologist of religion, Rodney Stark, told me that (until I asked) he had never heard of Schwarz or his book; several of Stark's peers said the same. Lyle Schaller, who knew more about churches than anyone else who ever lived, reported that he read *Natural Church Development* but immediately perceived it to be methodologically flawed—because its conclusions depend entirely upon the subjective self-reporting of core church members.

However, many pastors and other church leaders have sworn by it, and many denominational leaders have been captivated by Schwarz's church health paradigm. They reported that they found literature on church growth "too complicated," so they gravitated toward a resource that appeared to be a manual, even a recipe. They moved beyond Schwarz, however, in one serious way: Christian

---

2. See www.ncd-international.org.

3. NCD's website does not report, however, what percentage of the churches were already growing, or what percentage of those increased their growth rate to a statistically significant degree, or for how long, or how much of the growth represents actual converts from the world.

Schwarz never claimed that a church's quest for its own health is its main business; many church and judicatory leaders function as though the pursuit of church health *is* their main business. However, Schwarz did seem to assume that the end-goal is church growth; health leads to growth.

In time, many church leaders and denominations withdrew from Schwarz's eight essentials and developed their own profile of the features that, they believe, account for "church health." Many books, manuals, and articles have promoted their contrasting conclusions. At least one variation, the Anglican Diocese of London's "Seven Marks of a Healthy Church," shows remarkably little alignment with NCD's eight priority qualities.[4] The range, quality, and depth of the research behind these alternative profiles vary enormously; some may be based merely on leader-group preferences, with no research base at all! In all of the variations, the focus is on the church's own health.

What has survived among the many versions is one basic assumption that now goes beyond anything Schwarz actually claimed: what matters **most** is a church's *health*, then its growth, but not its outreach mission. So, across the Atlantic, the editors of *Church Growth Digest*—which was published in English for European church leaders for twenty-four years, announced in spring 2004 that their journal would hereafter be named *Healthy Church U.K.* By 2010, many church leaders on both sides of the Atlantic were speaking from the same script: "Church growth is passé; Church health has taken its place!" (The claim, of course, makes no more sense than to say that one's personal health has taken the place of one's vocation.)

---

4. See "Seven Marks of a Healthy Church," Diocese of London, www.london .anglican.org/kb/seven-marks-of-a-healthy-church/.

Our Main Business Not Essentially about "Health" *or* "Growth"

This book departs from both assumptions; the end-goal of the Christian movement is neither its own health nor its own growth. The end-goal is the Christian movement's enhanced witness and ministry to the world. The more transcendent goal is to help all people, by grace, to become the people they were meant to be and for God's will to be done on earth as it is in heaven.[5] The growth of churches should contribute more and more committed personnel for the movement's ministries and thereby expand the movement. While greater health may contribute to growth, greater health ultimately comes to churches as a by-product of obedience to the Great Commandment and the Great Commission *and* from a steady stream of new Christians entering a church's ranks.

It is important to report that the normative "church growth" literature is not primarily about numerical growth; the term is shorthand for several overlapping interests related to a church's mission: (1) The church growth movement encourages churches to rediscover their "main business" (i.e., the apostolic mandate to reach, serve, and disciple pre-Christian people). (2) Its literature exists to inform effective ministry and evangelism locally, and strategic mission globally. (3) Church growth people draw, in addition to scripture and theology, from historical and field studies to inform evangelism and

---

5. Biblical realism informs us that the kingdom that was initiated in Jesus's ministry will be consummated one day, in God's good time. In this interim time, we will never "build" God's kingdom, but we can cooperate with the Lord's revealed will and help bend history more in that direction. As one example among many, Christians once labored to abolish the slave trade, and then slavery. In this area, the world now more closely approximates the kingdom, though slavery, in altered forms like sexual trafficking and de facto labor slavery, still exists, and Christians still work to set people free.

mission; since membership trends can indicate a church's greater or lesser effectiveness, "the numbers" suggest where to do the research. (4) The field research informs us that what makes evangelism, ministry, and mission effective varies, sometimes enormously, from one people and context (such as Inuit people in Pond Inlet, Canada) to another people and context (such as Wall Street people in Manhattan); the literature helps church leaders to discover, in their field of mission, the ways to adapt, serve, and reach people.

Since Natural Church Development ignores such interests and only focuses on "church health," the claim that it has "taken the place of church growth" warrants a chuckle. NCD has little to say about effective evangelism, less about world mission, even less about adapting to host populations. While NCD has partner organizations in over sixty nations, they assume that the eight qualities are normative everywhere. While "church health" has not replaced church growth, it *has* substantially replaced the decades-long interest in "church renewal"—with most of the theology removed. Several critics have charged, with some exaggeration, that Church health is "church renewal lite"!

Even if the question is less than the ultimate question, does increased health lead to increased growth? NCD assures us that, as a church's core members can rate their church as increasingly healthy over time, the church's growth will necessarily follow; some studies, however, have discovered little correlation. For example, Phil Perkins's doctoral study of ten team-led Wesleyan churches, all scoring high on the "church health" indicators, showed that the ten churches, together, averaged somewhat less worship attendance and reported somewhat lower membership than five years earlier; even the six "most healthy" churches reported, together, statistically insignificant increases in attendance and membership.[6]

---

6. Phillip R. Perkins, "Pastoral Teams and Congregational Health in Smaller Churches" (DMiss. diss., Wilmore, KY: Asbury Theological Seminary, 2007), 283.

Two empirical researchers, John Ellas and Flavil Yeakley, published an independent statistical analysis of the NCD project in *The Journal of the America Society for Church Growth*.[7] That review, plus several discussions of NCD in the Society's meetings, has contributed the following observations:

How Original Is Natural Church Development?

Regarding Natural Church Development's claim to originality, some of the NCD team's work does represent some original, or fairly original, pioneering.

a) The NCD survey did take on a large, statistical, quantitative study of church health and growth, though it was *not* (as it claims) the *first* quantitative study (nor as "scientific" as it claims).

b) In a departure from the many church growth studies since the early 1970s, Natural Church Development focuses on church "health" more than most, though it was not the first, and NCD's allegation that church growth writers have been *un*interested in congregational health is not factual. "Internal" (or "quality") church growth has always been one of the four primary categories in the church growth lore, though people in Christian education, church renewal, and spiritual formation, and now NCD and other "church health" people, have contributed more to understanding and advancing quality growth.

_____

7. See the review of *Natural Church Development* by John Ellas and Flavil Yeakley, "A Review of *Natural Church Development* by Christian Swartz" in the *Journal of the American Society for Church Growth* (Spring, 1999), 83–91. In recent years, the Society has experienced a name change: The Great Commission Research Network. The journal, still published, is now titled *The Great Commission Research Journal.*

c) NCD's claim that a church experiences new health and growth by focusing most on its weaknesses among the eight qualities may be quite original; most scholars in organization leadership have advised organizations to identify, and build upon, their strengths. (The truth lurks, undoubtedly, somewhere in between. For instance, if a church's greatest comparative weakness is evangelism, the church would likely grow through more and better evangelism; but achieving a more "functional structure" might not, by itself, bring growth.)

d) Some NCD claims to *original* insight are not warranted. The chapter on Functional Structures, for instance, claims, "Our research confirmed for the first time an extremely negative relationship between traditionalism and both growth and quality within the church."[8] If, prior to NCD, this connection was a secret, it was a badly kept secret. Many leaders and scholars have observed the connection for many years.

e) In an apparent contradiction, NCD claims that, while "traditionalism" in a church's organizational life is not effective and must yield to functional structures, traditionalism is fully permissible in worship! So, Schwarz says, "Services may target Christians or non-Christians, their style may be liturgical or free, their language may be 'churchy' or secular—it makes no difference for church growth."[9] The more nuanced fact is that, for most pre-Christian populations, in most places, congregations that welcome seekers, and begin where they are, and employ language and music and other cultural forms that they understand, do engage more pre-Christian people and experience much more conversion growth from the world than traditional churches, though the most effective traditional churches more often retain their own children and experience transfer growth.

---

8. *Natural Church Development*, 28.
9. Ibid., 30.

What Can We Really Know from NCD's Research?

a) The original NCD study gathered, from thirty people in one thousand churches, the self-perceptions of core members about their churches, and then assumed that core-member self-perceptions are "facts." At least three types of cases suggest otherwise: (1) A local church's Builder Generation members might experience an organ interlude from Bach as "inspiring worship"; but younger pre-Christian visitors, raised more on rock than Bach, might not. (2) Core members may report "loving relationships" within their fellowship; a newcomer single woman with a child, an addiction, and a reputation might not experience the fellowship the same way. (3) Less hypothetical, John Ellas distributed the NCD survey instrument in the congregation he attends. He reports: "Members' perceptions of congregational strengths were highly inaccurate in numerous categories." For instance, members rated their church's "need-oriented evangelism" fourth highest among the characteristics; Ellas reports, however, that the church had no notable evangelism emphasis in the preceding five years, and it experienced less than half the conversion growth rate we typically observe in growing churches.[10]

b) *Natural Church Development* does not provide enough data or detail for other researchers to replicate the study, nor even enough data to understand the basis of the conclusions.

c) The book does not report the statistical significance level of its conclusions; without knowing the significance level, statisticians tell us, no statistical study should be relied upon.

d) The study claims to present the universal *causes* of church

10.   Ellas and Yeakley, "A Review of *Natural Church Development*," 90–91.

health and growth, but it only presents *correlations*—which are alleged, but not sufficiently demonstrated. Some (or most) of the eight qualities *might*, indeed, produce church health and growth. However, the reverse could happen; the experience of growth may produce the climate in which members have more positive perceptions of some (or all) of the eight NCD qualities. Again, both the health and the growth may come (at least partly) from other causes, as I will suggest below.

e) NCD passes off, as original, some insights which are *not* original, and without citing the sources whose insights they repeat. For example, Win Arn demonstrated in the early 1980s, from surveys in hundreds of churches, the correlation between the people's perceptions of love (toward each other in the church *and* toward the outside community) and the church's growth.[11] (I am informed that Christian Schwarz was first schooled in these matters by time spent with Win Arn and his organization.)

f) Ellas and Yeakley reported that, after seven years of NCD's ten-year study, a consultant identified several serious flaws in their instrument and their testing procedure. To NCD's credit, they fixed the instrument and the procedure; they based their conclusions, however, on the data from the whole ten years![12]

g) Most church growth researchers would say that NCD's methods fall shortest at two points.

First, they neglected to survey *new converts*—who are, after all, the population pool most capable of telling how and why they were attracted, and experienced faith, and joined the church; the

11. Win Arn, Carroll Nyquist, and Charles Arn, *Who Cares About Love?* (Pasadena, CA: Church Growth Press, 1986).
12. Ellas and Yeakley, "A Review of *Natural Church Development*," (Spring, 1999), 86–87.

pastor and established members, often, only think they know why their church is growing. (For example, pastors more often attribute their church's growth to their preaching than do their church's converts!)

Second, NCD relied excessively on numbers crunching from questionnaires; only interviews, however, can confirm the people's understanding of the questions; only interviews can probe deeply enough to access people's experience; only interviews can probe people's tacit knowledge that they may have not yet verbalized; and only interviews (with skilled field observation) can identify many of the real causes of vitality, growth, and effective ministry.

What Do We Do with NCD's Conclusions?

a) Many church leaders do not know what to do with NCD's main claim that increased church health will bring church growth, because the book does not distinguish between the three ways that a church grows—biological growth, transfer growth, and conversion growth. This blur may help account for their claim that a service's style or target population makes no difference for church growth. It may make little difference in transfer growth; indeed, many "mobile Christians" prefer to join another liturgically traditional church. In secular societies, however, not many churches reach pre-Christian people without that being their purpose and without engaging in the strategic adjustments that help engage them.

Moreover, worship style does make a significant difference, virtually everywhere and at two levels, in a church's missionary outreach to pre-Christian populations. First, the public leadership and performance of worship needs to be engaging and varied enough to gain and retain the shorter attention span of this generation. It needs to at least be stimulating and interesting for a generation accustomed to being entertained. It needs to approach the level of precision and excellence they experience from television, concerts, theater, and performers. The rise of TED Talks has demonstrated that it is possible to communicate significant ideas, to a non-specialized audience, in eighteen minutes. By comparison, the performance of the announcements, prayers, and sermons in most churches drowns most good ideas in a flood of excess verbiage. If the service is "bush league," most seekers won't be back.

Second, regarding the issue of music, it is difficult to find churches experiencing significant conversion growth from the world through, say, classical music—although one congregation of Redeemer Presbyterian Church in Manhattan is a notable exception because, in Manhattan's large population, a substantial population understands and loves classical music; and, for a similar reason, another Redeemer congregation features Jazz. In any case, effective outreaching churches do *not* do that traditional music "the same old way." They invest the music with greater energy and complexity, they follow a revised composition, or they improvise; they accompany it with "contemporary" instrumentation; and the "old music" is thereby experienced as powerfully "contemporary." (For example, listen to the Brooklyn Tabernacle Choir's rendition of the Halleluiah Chorus of Handel's *Messiah*.)

b) The chapter on "Loving Relationships" in *Natural Church Development* reflects little knowledge of what *agape* love means in the New Testament. While NCD reports that they used a dozen variables in assessing the love in churches, the only two featured in the book—laughter in the church and spending time together—do not necessarily indicate the presence of *agapaic* love, especially love for lost people. Christian love is, undoubtedly, an essential feature

121

of healthy growing churches, but NCD does not demonstrate it.

c) NCD's people do their project a disservice by the device of attaching one, and only one, adjective to each quality. Truth is seldom that simple, and what is going on is seldom that singular. For instance, most leadership studies indicate that it is as important for leaders to be "visionary" and "collaborative" as to be "empowering," and surely "faithful" and "obedient" are at least as important in spirituality as "passionate." Again, devotees of Saddleback Church's SHAPE acronym (Spiritual gifts, Heart, Abilities, Personality type, and Experiences) are convinced that discovering one's spiritual giftedness, alone, is less empowering for ministry than a more comprehensive understanding of how the Holy Spirit has "shaped" people for ministry.

d) In some cases, the favored adjective overstates what NCD has demonstrated. For instance, NCD reports a greater correlation between "small groups" and church growth than for any of the other seven characteristics. *But*, they say, the groups must be "holistic." Curiously, NCD says small groups are "holistic" *if* they study the Bible *and* apply it to their lives (regardless, apparently, of whether they pray, or welcome seekers into the group, or have any ministry or cause outside the group, or whether they even minister to each other—which many majority world church leaders tell us is the supreme reason for small group life.)

e) So NCD may often be mistaken to emphasize any one adjective more than the noun it modifies. It is more strategic to emphasize the nouns, and to nuance each noun with the one-to-several adjectives that do fuller justice to the characteristic than one adjective, alone, can do. Albert Einstein advised knowledge leaders, "We must make everything as simple as possible, but not simpler." The church health folks have made it simpler than is possible.

If It's Really about Christianity's Mission, Consider Eight Themes

NCD assumes, without sufficient warrant, that their eight characteristics are *the* eight characteristics of healthy growing churches. It is possible, however, to identify other characteristics that are *at least* as normative for a church's health, growth, *and* its mission as the eight that NCD emphasizes. Consider the following:

1. **Macro-Context.** In the long study of Christian mission, the greatest consensus relates to a mission's context. To effectively reach and serve a people, and grow among them to reach and serve still more people, the Christian movement *must* adapt to the specific historical and cultural context. The faith serves and spreads differently in nomadic desert settlements than in mountain villages or arctic communities, and still differently in Moscow, or Chicago, or Sao Paulo. The faith serves and spreads differently among non-literate peoples than formally educated peoples, among refugees than suburbanites, and differently among peoples with a vivid sense of the supernatural than among secularized peoples. Mission scholars know that to ignore the general contexts, and then assume we can "do church" the same way everywhere, is folly.

   Indeed, the definitive studies of effective organizations, of all kinds—from fast-food restaurants to automobile manufacturers to computer software companies to universities—substantially attribute their effectiveness to their understanding of, and strategic adaptation to, their general context, and to that context's ongoing changes. Long term, *all* effective organizations are "open systems";[13] to serve and

---

13.   I have expanded on the "open system" theory of effective organizations in chapter three of *The Recovery of a Contagious Methodist Movement* (Nashville: Abingdon Press, 2011). *The Celtic Way of Evangelism* (Nashville: Abingdon, 2000, rev. ed. 2010) shows how the principles help account for the spread of the greatest sustained

123

reach the wider community, they study and adapt to that community. The NCD approach, however, features no need to understand the "soils" in which we are called to plant the gospel seed.

2. **Culture.** NCD disregards, likewise, a supremely important part of any church's context—the culture of the target population. We are certain, from a long history of mission studies, that culturally "indigenous" communication and ministry removes false stumbling blocks, and makes it possible to engage the people of any society, in any and every field of mission. An indigenous strategy requires paying the price to understand the language and the customs, and the typical beliefs, attitudes, values, and general worldview of the host population's shared consciousness. The assumption that a church can effectively reach and serve a population without understanding their culture is delusional.[14]

3. **Credibility.** The credibility of a church with a pre-Christian population is, undoubtedly, more important than any characteristic that NCD features. Helmut Thielicke observed, in the secular West Germany of the mid-twentieth century that the single most important variable in whether or not the people will take Christianity's message seriously is the perceived credibility of the witnessing community.[15] The academic study of communication has known, for twenty-three centuries, that the perceived credibility of an advocate powerfully affects the message's reception. My own field research with secular people, beginning in 1962, persistently indicates that, in great numbers, they want to know (a)

---

mission in Christianity's history. *How to Reach Secular People* (Nashville: Abingdon, 1992) and *Should We Change Our Game Plan?* (Nashville: Abingdon, 2013) feature strategic adaptation to the West's secular contexts.

14. If this challenge seems daunting, there is a workbook for you! See Craig Storti, *Figuring Foreigners Out: A Practical Guide* (Yarmouth, ME: Intercultural Press, 2011).

15. See Helmut Thielicke, *The Trouble with the Church* (New York: Harper and Row, 1965), especially 1–11.

whether we really believe it, (b) and/or whether we live by it, (c) and/or whether it makes enough difference for them to take it seriously.

4. **Outreach Ministry.** You would never know for sure, from NCD, whether healthy growing churches are *in ministry* to pre-Christian people *and* are sharing the gospel. You could infer this from the quality they name "Need-oriented Evangelism," but the term may obscure as much as it reveals.

   In any case, more and more of the earth's contagious churches are reaching pre-Christian people through outreach ministries—from GED tutoring, to literacy classes, to teaching English, to a range of support groups and recovery ministries, to food, clothing, medical, dental, counseling, and countless other ministries. But two distinctions need to be made. First, outreach ministries do not require people to become Christians; a ministry gladly administers a flu shot, or teaches someone to read, whether they become disciples or not. Second, that policy—service without a hook, enhances the church's public credibility for witness. Since people are more than souls with ears, witness within ministry reaches more people than witness alone.

5. **Social Ethic.** The NCD model seems to assume that a church can be "healthy" without a social ethic. NCD's model of a "healthy church" includes no priority concern for justice, or peace, or reconciliation between peoples, or for human health, or creation's health. A team of Christian leaders from Germany (of all places) appears to have gained no enduring insight from their people's experience of the Third Reich, the Holocaust, and World War II.

   Let's recall some of what once happened. In 1936, Adolph Hitler was elected Fuehrer, and the Third Reich took over. New laws required Germany's churches to submit complete copies of their baptismal and membership records. The churches, with few exceptions, complied. The government then used the church rosters to identify the people who were "Aryan"; people not on the master list were presumed to not be members of the master race. The government then targeted Jewish and Gypsy populations for prison camps and exterminations. Some of the German churches that slept through the 1930s, who complied with a totalitarian regime and expressed no public prophetic challenge to serious evil would have scored high on NCD's health questionnaire! How "healthy" can that kind of Christianity really be?

6. **Strength in the denominational tradition**. The NCD model, while providing a generic model for churches of any denomination, ignores the fact that fidelity and strength in the integrity of a church's tradition is also a sign of health. So, for example, how "healthy" is a Lutheran church that does not feature justification, or a Quaker church that is not engaged in peacemaking? Many denominations have recognized that, to some degree, "health" is denomination-specific, and they have developed healthy church profiles that contrast with NCD's. For instance, the Evangelical Free Church's research (www.efca.org) produced "Ten Leading Indicators" of church health. Two—"Passionate Spirituality" and "Loving Relationships"—replicated NCD's qualities exactly. Two others—"Fruitful Evangelism" and "High Impact Worship"—replicated an NCD noun, with a different adjective. EFC's other six indicators were not featured in NCD's profile.

7. **Local Contextual Factors**. There are *always* local contextual factors that need to be included in any useful profile of a healthy church. Recent folk wisdom has suggested that "all politics is local"; Christianity is necessarily local. If, say, the church's immediate ministry area has been "swamped" by a hurricane, or crime, or job losses, or a shooting at the nearby school, or by Haitian immigrants, each local church needs the latitude to shape the model of its effectiveness in terms of the challenges, opportunities, and "harvest" within the immediate context. Indeed, local contexts vary so

significantly that a recipe or manual that will fit every local situation is impossible to produce. Most effective churches have some objectives that are tailored specifically to local contexts—from Brooklyn, New York, to Baker Lake, Nunavut Territory.

8. **The Wider Mission**. The NCD model seems to assume that a church can be "healthy" without a wider mission. But how "healthy" can a church be without a deep involvement in Christ's wider mission, nationally and globally? Would we reasonably expect the God we know, through the biblical revelation, to bless a local church whose range of compassionate concern stops at the city limits?

Reflections from the Past and Present

Since releasing an earlier version of this chapter, I have heard from many church leaders who tried the Natural Church Development approach and found it wanting. The case of a church with a weekly attendance of 1,100 in Maryland is fairly typical. The senior pastor took all of NCD's seminars and received their "certification." He then launched an NCD campaign in his church. He recruited thirty core members to fill out the NCD questionnaire. When the pastor studied the results, he knew they were skewed beyond uselessness. The church scored highest in gift-oriented ministries; the pastor discerned, immediately, that *those thirty* people knew their gifts and were involved in ministry, but the vast majority of the members did not and were not. He discerned that the questionnaire data also misrepresented the congregation, as a whole, in several other traits.

I am concerned that the NCD approach to "church health" repeats five of the Big Mistakes of the past.

1. NCD misperceives outreach as only one of eight priorities of the congregation. Churches in the tradition of the apostles see ministry-based evangelism as their priority business. Then, as the movement reaches more people, it deploys more people in more ministries.

2. NCD fails to perceive that the church's lack of obedience in outreach is often the most important cause of the church's pathology; so it is futile to work on health without outreach.

3. NCD reinforces the tendency in all churches to turn inward—in endless self-preoccupation and self-analysis; by contrast, apostolic congregations mainly focus outward, on human need and "the harvest."

4. Many churches influenced by some version of the NCD model perpetuate the older assumption that if a local church can only get "renewed" or "healthy" enough, *then* it can, and will, reach out effectively; actually, churches that adopt the "renewal first" strategy seldom get around to much outreach, because they *never* feel healthy or renewed enough to move on to the next phase.

5. Neither the church renewal people nor the church health people have discovered what is obvious to most church growth researchers: churches are renewed more from a steady stream of new Christians entering their ranks than from all the known renewal ministries, combined.

Affirmations of Natural Church Development

There is much worth affirming in the wide interest in "church health," and specifically in the *Natural Church Development* project. NCD's leaders want churches to experience greater health (and growth), and they launched an ambitious undertaking to give church health and growth a clearer rationale and a better footing. Some of their conclusions are surely valid, though because of problems with the research instrument, the population surveyed, and the interpretation, we cannot with certitude say which! Many church leaders are undoubtedly attracted to NCD's eight characteristics—largely, I suggest, because themes like "inspiring worship" and "loving relationships" confirm what many church leaders have intuitively believed all along! NCD's popularity is also partly due to a remarkable assumption: most of this "scientific research" confirms Christian folk-wisdom! Furthermore, many church leaders will buy *anything* that claims to be "scientific, "organic," or "natural."

Some churches are undoubtedly helped by NCD's model—in part because they believe in it enough to plan and act upon it. The implementation of a local church's NCD plan acts, at least, like the "placebo" effect in medical studies—in which (say) blood pressure improves almost as much in the experimental control subjects who took the placebo as in those who took the experimental drug. So we are grateful to NCD for the churches that believe in it enough to get an act together. We are grateful to NCD for whatever they now hypothesize that ultimately turns out to be true. We are grateful to NCD for the visibility they have given, in some quarters, to issues of church health and church growth.

We are also grateful to NCD for provoking some of us in the church growth school of thought into a new period of field research, reflection, and clarification, and for the reminder to make church growth lore "as simple as possible." We resist the temptation, however, to make it "simpler" than is possible—while sympathizing with busy church leaders who crave greater simplicity in a world of complexity. After all, reaching a lost soul, like raising a teenager or maintaining a marriage or investing in stocks, "ought" to be simpler than it is; and reaching a pre-Christian society, like advancing literacy or defeating an epidemic or bringing democracy to the Middle East and peace on earth, "ought" to be simpler than it is.

We know, however, that the courageous minority who look complexity, in the teeth, who pay an intellectual price to understand it and then translate it for non-specialists, informs most of the advances in human affairs. We still do not know how to reduce the whole corpus of church growth lore to as much simplicity as many leaders would want (although the next chapter takes a step in that direction). We can, however, now identify the 20 percent of church growth knowledge that accounts for about 80 percent of the difference; this was the purpose of my fairly recent book *The Apostolic Congregation*. But, for reasons explained above, we cannot make things simpler than is possible. Leaders who are unwilling to love the Lord of the Harvest with their minds (as well as their hearts) will be unable to appropriate much of what can now be known about serving and reaching people, and leading local movements.

One More Reservation and One More Affirmation of a European Import

I have saved my most serious reservation about the Natural Church Development project for next to last. I have mentioned that European Christian leaders were excited about NCD because it wasn't "imported from America." Fair enough, but how wise were the American church leaders who quickly adopted this import from Europe? NCD is, after all, rooted in European Christianity, more specifically European state-church Christianity (and Europe's *slightly* reformed "Free Churches"). NCD assumes, remarkably, that nothing is seriously wrong with the traditional European state-church way of "doing church"; so the only interventions needed are at a relatively surface level, like making the structure more "functional" or making the worship service more "inspiring."

I wish that NCD's major assumption was valid, because we can know how they "did church" back (say) in seventeenth-century Scotland; so if we could repeat that forever (only better), we could get "church" right every time! The problem, of course, is that most of the traditional European churches have not gathered appreciable harvests for decades.

Furthermore, there are no reasons to share European Christianity's entrenched assumption that European institutional state-church Christianity is pretty much what Jesus and the original apostles had in mind. What they did have in mind, and modeled, was a much less "institutional" and a much more "movemental" and "apostolic" way of doing church, which I have already suggested from Luke's Gospel and explored in several books.[16]

I have saved my most serious affirmation of NCD for last. In many minds, their focus on eight qualities has given a generation of church leaders an "assumptions transplant." When I was young, many churches "majored" on **one** thing; they virtually assumed that if a church was really good at one thing, it was a notable church. So the leaders mastered one thing, and let local experience and denominational folk-wisdom inform everything else they did. In Miami, Florida, where I was raised, one church had a "great Sunday school," another was noted for Bible teaching, and others for their choir, or annual revival, or children's ministry, or youth ministry, or women's ministry. (No church was known for reaching and serving men.) A church's distinction shaped its "image" in the community,

---

16. See George G. Hunter, III, *How to Reach Secular People* (Nashville: Abingdon, 1992), *Church for the Unchurched* (Nashville: Abingdon, 1996), *The Celtic Way of Evangelism* (Nashville: Abingdon, 2000), *Radical Outreach: The Recovery of Apostolic Ministry and Evangelism* (Nashville: Abingdon, 2003), and *The Apostolic Congregation: Church Growth Reconceived for a New Generation* (Nashville: Abingdon, 2009).

and a church's "image" mattered. Many people were attracted to a church that was known for something good. Likewise, many people were repelled from churches known for conflict, dogmatism, self-righteousness, or "always asking for money!"

Now, the current and rising generations of church leaders often share a different assumption. They assume that an effective church, especially in secular communities, must be competent at many things. Natural Church Development has catalyzed that paradigm shift more than any other known cause.

So, a church's leaders, as a group, might need **sufficient** knowledge and competence in scripture, church history, theology, and ethics; in worship, preaching, and music, with background knowledge of aesthetics and rhetoric; and in leadership, management, and the dynamics of a volunteer organization; in group life, lay ministries, and a range of outreach ministries; in local history, culture, and demographics; in evangelism and mission; in catechesis, Christian education, spiritual formation, and renewal; and more. No one becomes an "expert" in all of that, but a church's practices are now informed by the best insights from such a range of fields. In an age of complexity and knowledge explosion, mere folk wisdom lacks enough insight to inform much effectiveness. While this may sound daunting, the following story should put the challenge of knowledge-leadership for the church in perspective.

A Parable for Twenty-First-Century Church Leaders

Natural Public Radio once featured a fellow who made a similar discovery. He was a PhD in botany, a professor at an eastern university. On vacation in England one summer, he fell in love with "great Victorian gardens."

Returning home, he decided to retire somewhat early to turn the acreage behind his home into a Victorian garden paradise. How hard could it be? After all, he had three degrees in Botany.

Several years into his project, his garden showed little resemblance to *any* "great Victorian garden" in England. There were some lovely plants and pretty flowers here and there, but an almost endless series of surprises—like inconsistent rainfall, and the occasional drought, and insects and pests and plant diseases of many species—had sabotaged his dream. And the hummingbirds and songbirds that reveled in Victorian gardens had snubbed the botanist's garden.

Our hero returned to England, revisited the gardens, and this time he interviewed the head gardeners. This was his eureka discovery: every "great Victorian garden" has at least one great Victorian gardener!

He discovered that he knew more botany than they did, though they knew more about the specific plant species that populated their gardens; three degrees in botany had not taught him enough about primroses. He also discovered that they "knew stuff" about geology, soils, climate, weather, insects, birds, bees, weeds, trees, worms, and a dozen other quite specific bodies of knowledge; they were not experts, but they were informed. He learned that he had to integrate branches of practical knowledge, like learning the plants that attract hummingbirds. And he learned that all of this 101-level knowledge had to be specific for his "bioregion."

The botanist's experience is a parable for effective church leadership for today and tomorrow. Leaders tap into broad bodies of knowledge to inform their church's strategy and approach to ministry; effective churches now become effective at a range of things. The lead pastor does not master all of this; local Christianity is a team game. The church relies on informed volunteers, staff people, outside experts, and networking with other churches—like a head gardener may rely on the local TV weatherman for next week's forecast and an entomologist for upping his game in pest control.

Church leadership is especially like gardening in two ways.

First, things change, surprises happen, and there is always much to learn; that is one reason why, for those of us who are wired and called this way, church leadership is the most interesting vocation in the solar system.

Second, neither a garden nor a church will ever be exactly like you (or God) want it; it is always a wondrous work in process.

A Church's Main Business: Theological and Strategic Views

T his book encourages a Really Big Idea that was once the driving priority of the early Christian movement, but now seems like a new, even absurd, idea to most Christians to-day. In the followers of Jesus, the High God of Israel raised up a movement to bring salvation and shalom to the earth's peoples. Early Christians were clear that they were the salt of the earth, ambassadors for Christ, who would appeal to all people to be reconciled to God, to experience the life they were meant for, and to be agents of God's will. In this paradigm, Christianity's main business is not taking care of the people we already have, as important as that is; the main business is its mission to the world. The church is not only an Ecclesia—the called-out people of God; it is also an Apostolate—the sent-out people of God.

This apostolic vision is rooted in the ancient promise to Abraham—that, in his descendants, God would shape a people who would "bless" all of the earth's peoples. When that nation misinterpreted their calling, they protected the revelation from contamination by the neighboring "barbarians." So God raised up a new people who understood that the revelation was for the sake of the "barbarians!"[1] This New Israel, constituted by a shared faith rather than a shared bloodline, was to fulfill Christ's Great Commission—to "find," and make disciples among, the "lost" peoples of the earth. Leander Keck, dean of Yale Divinity School, used to challenge Christians to spend their lives offering the gospel to people—because "the gospel is the only thing we have to offer the world that it does not already have."[2]

Theology and Strategy

In the 1970s, Donald McGavran's church growth school of thought, within mission studies, emerged to serve this apostolic vision. McGavran believed that every human being on earth has the inalienable "human right" to have the opportunity to become a Christ follower. Extending this right is so important that, if we do everything else we can for people except for that, we ultimately fail them. This ministry is so important that we must study the churches that are already receiving new Christians "from the world," because some of those churches are the Lord's living laboratories and demonstration centers. We can often learn from them the approaches that are reproducible or adaptable to other ministry areas where the biblical harvest is ripe, but the laborers have not yet discovered how to enter or gather it. McGavran believed that it is God's will that the church grows as lost people are found.[3]

It became fashionable, however, for some desk theologians to announce that church growth simply "lacks...a theological and

---

1. I develop this metaphor of mission to the "barbarians" in *The Celtic Way of Evangelism,* revised edition (Nashville: Abingdon, 2010).

2. This quotation is from my notes on a lecture Keck gave in an Atlanta evangelism symposium in 1999.

3. Donald A. McGavran, with C. Peter Wagner, "God's Will and Church Growth," in *Understanding Church Growth,* 3rd ed. (Grand Rapids, MI: Wm. B. Eerdmans, 1990), 20–30.

scriptural basis."[4] Au contraire! One has to avoid reading the scriptures, or read them through very filtered lenses, to maintain that fiction.

Actually, some very notable theologians were seriously committed to the spread of the faith. Kenneth Scott Latourette, the twentieth century's foremost church historian, devoted his life to writing a seven-volume *History of the Expansion of Christianity*.[5] Oscar Cullman's *Christ and Time* contended that *the* paradigm of the New Testament writers viewed the church as living in the "expansionary" phase of God's redemptive design.[6]

Emil Brunner famously declared, "The Church exists for mission as a fire exists by burning.... Where there is no mission, there is no Church, and where there is neither church nor mission, there is no faith."[7] William Temple observed, "The Church is the only society on earth that exists for the benefit of non-members." C. S. Lewis declared, "The Church exists for nothing else but to draw men into Christ, to make them little Christs. If they are not doing that, all the cathedrals, clergy, missions, sermons, even the Bible itself, are simply a waste of time. God became Man for no other purpose. It is even doubtful, you know, whether the whole universe was created for any other purpose."[8]

---

4. See Elaine A. Robinson, *Godbearing: Evangelism Reconceived* (Cleveland, OH: The Pilgrim Press, 2006), 70. Robinson does not cite, much less interact with, any church growth sources.

5. Latourette summarized his strategic insights in the first volume.

6. In the first phase of redemptive history, God's involvement began with all humanity and in time narrowed to one nation, then to a remnant of that nation, then to One Man—the second Adam; from that One Man, the expansion began—to the twelve, then 70 and 120, then 3,000 and 5,000, to Jerusalem, Judea, Samaria, and to the ends of the earth and to all peoples. Some of Cullman's later interpreters doubted that he had sufficiently demonstrated that *every* New Testament writer saw reality through this paradigm, but they conceded that, at least, the author of Luke-Acts did.

7. H. Emil Brunner, *The Word and the World* (London: SCM Press, 1931), 108.

8. C. S. Lewis, *Mere Christianity* (San Francisco, CA: HarperSanFrancisco, 2001), 199.

The church growth school of thought, however, has not "majored" in constructive theology. With most other Christians, we regard Christian truth as revealed, we are grounded in the gospel, and we affirm the classical theology of the church, with deep roots in the scriptures and normative respect for the ancient creeds. Church growth leaders have seldom presumed to improve on "the faith once delivered to the saints!"

Furthermore, church growth people usually identify with one of the Protestant theological traditions. Roman Catholic mission scholars, however, surfaced as fellow travelers and contributors. Vincent Donovan's *Christianity Rediscovered*,[9] his reflection on planting Catholic churches among the Masai people of East Africa, may be our greatest case study.

Furthermore, because church growth is a field within the broader study of Christian mission, we generally share the mission theology of our colleagues. Church growth has not primarily contributed to theology because theology, per se, is not our main business, and speculative theology is not the arena for our essential contribution. If the reflection behind important human (including Christian) activity functions within a theology—strategy—practice spectrum, church growth's essential contribution is located squarely in the middle, while drawing from theology and reflecting upon effective practice, with some contribution to theology and more to practice.

Specifically, church growth's main business and indispensable contribution has been to discover, in that middle strategic level, answers to two serious questions. These two questions are so important that, if we devoted our main attention to theology instead of these two questions, we would neglect our essential contribution. *Many* Christian leaders do theology in the service of church and academy. Many more practice ministry with Christians and even with pre-Christian people. Very few Christian leaders engage the strategic

9. (Maryknoll, NY: Orbis Press, 1979).

middle between theory and practice. Indeed, church growth thinkers have addressed two questions that virtually no one was even asking, much less finding answers to.

The First Serious Question: Effective Evangelism

The first question, reflected in the title of Donald McGavran's last major book, expresses the quest for *Effective Evangelism.* How does the gospel spread between persons, among a people, and from one people to another? How do we communicate the meaning of the gospel to people who do not even know what we are talking about? How do people become Christians? How can we help them become Christians? The communication of Christianity, with the hope that people will respond and become disciples, is a formidable challenge for any communicator or movement leader.

Believe it or not, such questions have seldom been asked in Christianity's most recent millennium. A very few reflective practitioners, such as Jonathan Edwards, John Wesley,[10] Charles G. Finney, and Charles Spurgeon, observed their times and their target populations, interviewed converts, reflected on their ministry, asked how it could be more effective, risked innovations, and pioneered new approaches published their insights. In our colleges and seminaries, teachers of scripture, church history, and theology have usually ignored the strategic questions.[11] Teachers of worship, preaching,

---

10.   See my book *To Spread the Power: Church Growth in the Wesleyan Spirit* (Nashville: Abingdon Press, 1987).

11.   Over the years, several notable theologians have told me that such questions are "beneath" them! The first chapter of Fred Craddock's *Overhearing the Gospel,* rev. and ex. ed. (St. Louis: Chalice Press, 2002) make a powerful case for taking "method" more seriously. This book, reflecting some from Kierkegaard, is one of the few great books on the effective communication of Christianity's message, and it anticipated the challenge of engaging post-modern people.

counseling, and Christian education have focused on more effective ministry to Christians, assuming that what engages Christians *should* also engage pre-Christian people.

In the history of the practice of evangelism, we seem to have hoped that we'd get it right the first time, because however we started out doing it is how we usually continued to do it for the next generation, or the next century, or more! If, say, camp meetings, or revivals, or crusades, or confirmation classes, or Bible distributions, or billboards, or "the Roman Road," or "the Four Spiritual Laws," or radio programs, or TV programs, or distributing gospel tracts once yielded any converts, we have assumed that is *the* way to do evangelism, everywhere and always! We have seldom asked McGavran's question: *Why* do we often come out of ripe harvest fields empty handed?

Many church leaders are allergic to self-critique. That is one reason why Donald McGavran's career, in the service of effective evangelism, was such a significant departure. McGavran, and the academic school within mission study that he launched, brought the rigor of *critique* to evangelization—across, and within, cultures. With appropriate respect for what we assumed we already knew, McGavran dared to ask: We know how the gospel ought to spread, but how does it really spread? We know how people ought to become Christians, but how do they actually become Christians? McGavran, with others, devoted decades of field research to such questions, observing Christian movements and interviewing first-generation converts. The discoveries of this field research tradition did ratify some Christian folklore, but it challenged some of it too, and produced some counterintuitive insights. For example:

1. The gospel spreads most contagiously not between strangers, nor by mass evangelism nor through mass media but along the lines of the kinship and friendship *networks* of credible Christians, especially new Christians.

2. The gospel spreads more easily to persons and peoples who are in a *receptive* season of their lives, and church growth research has discovered many indicators of likely receptive people.[12]

3. The gospel spreads more naturally among a people through their language, and the *indigenous* forms of their culture, than through alien languages or cultural forms.

4. First-generation groups, classes, choirs, congregations, churches, and ministries, and other *new units*, are more reproductive than old established units.

5. Apostolic ministry is more effective when we target *affinity groups* than when we merely target individuals on the one hand, or political units or geographic areas on the other.

Furthermore, church growth research has resulted in many more specific insights about effective evangelism. For instance...

1. Most effective evangelism does not involve a one-way presentation of the gospel but rather a two-way *conversation* about the gospel, and about the Christian faith more broadly, and about the Christian life.

2. Most effective evangelism involves *multiple* conversations over time.

3. Most effective conversations about the gospel involve the meaningful *interpretation* of the gospel.

4. In evangelical conversations, the gospel advocate's active *listening* is as important as what the advocate says; indeed, what the advocate hears influences what he or she then says.

---

12. See chapter 4 of Hunter, *The Apostolic Congregation: Church Growth Reconceived for a New Generation* (Nashville: Abingdon, 2009) for an explanation of fourteen guidelines for finding more receptive people than most church leaders ever dreamed were out there!

5. Most single episodes in effective evangelism do not attempt to present the whole gospel (which would storm people with "information overload") but features the one or two *facets* of the multifaceted gospel gem that are most relevant to the people's questions, needs, issues, and struggles.

6. Most cases of effective evangelism do not involve a single person who commends the gospel to a seeker; *several persons* serve as a person's bridges into faith, reminiscent of Paul's report, "I planted, Apollos watered, but God made it grow" (1 Cor 3:6).

7. So understood, evangelism is a *process*, rather than a single event, that the Holy Spirit is orchestrating in the life of a person or a people group. We are privileged to be involved as the Holy Spirit's junior partners in this process.

8. The evangelism process typically involves (say) thirty *experiences over time*. Some of the many links in the chain of experiences that leads to faith and new life are experiences—like experiencing the Holy Spirit in a worship experience, or observing a credible Christian in action, or an experience of answered prayer; as the would-be convert (say) is reflecting on Christian truth claims and biblical texts, reading books, attending Bible studies, asking questions, and trying to pray, she or he is contributing some of the links in the chain. So the experiences that lead to faith include, but are seldom limited to, what the evangelizers do with seekers.

9. The Holy Spirit is present not only in the witnessing Christian and in the gospel transactions but has already been with the Seeker, preparing him or her to be receptive to the gospel and experience life change. Effective outreach ministry builds on what we discover, through prayer, that the Spirit has been, and is, doing.

10. Evangelism probably includes, essentially, an appropriate *invitation* to receive and follow Christ through his church.

Though many people do not respond immediately when invited (the ball lies in their court for a while), many people do not consider responding without invitation.

11. Often, *multiple invitations* are necessary to help the person respond; each stage in the "adoption process" takes time and, often, seekers need to know that the church (and God) really wants them.

12. Increasingly, most people do not first become believers and then become involved with the church. More and more, "belonging comes before believing"; their involvement with a group or a congregation usually comes first, and they discover faith *through* their involvement in the community of faith. So "assimilation" often precedes belief and commitment; Christian faith is often "more caught than taught."

13. Increasingly, we observe, neither the Sunday school nor the gathered congregation will be the initial port of entry for many secular seekers; not even a "contemporary seekers service" will be an effective port of entry for many pagans. More and more pre-Christian people will be initially reached through a *group* or an "*outreach ministry*"—such as an interest group, support group, recovery ministry, and so forth. More and more, effective outreach is "ministry-based evangelism." More new people now enter through "side doors" rather than the "front door."

14. The essential task of evangelism is not so much the presenting of, say, traditionally faithful gospel words as the *communication* of the gospel's *meaning* to people in their words, in their life situation.

15. We are now much more aware that the communication process is enormously more *complex* than merely the accurate "presenting" of faithful information. Communication involves such factors as the perceived credibility of the witnesser (and the witnessing community); the "body

language" of the communicator; the relationship between the communicator and receptor; the images, attitudes, feelings, and cultural worldview the receptor brings to transactions; whether the receptor feels wanted, respected, and understood; the cultural relevance of the church's style, language, aesthetics, and music; the emotional impressions created by the ministries, music, message, and architecture; how interesting we present the possibility; and a host of other known (and unknown) communication variables.

Most of all, perhaps, our research has demonstrated that there is no one approach or method of evangelization that, like a stretch sock, will fit every situation! So the church growth school teaches Christian leaders how to discover, in their situation, the available means to engage and serve the people, communicate the message, invite response, and ground and shape new disciples.

The Second Serious Question: Effective Mission

The second essential issue that church growth addressed, once widely ignored, focuses on mission strategy. How do we help make cross-cultural mission both faithful and effective? The task of engaging and serving a population, communicating the gospel, planting and expanding a Christian movement, and working for a more just and peaceful society, and all of that in a different tongue and cultural context, is immeasurably more formidable than outreach within one's own culture. Historically, some impressive leaders have engaged in critique and strategic thinking in this second issue. Names like Patrick, Gregory, Boniface, Bartholomew de Las Casas, Robert de Nobili, Matteo Ricci, Ignatius of Loyola, Francis Xavier, William Carey, Rufus Anderson, Henry Venn, and Roland Allen come to mind. Yet many of these strategic mission thinkers were ignored in their own time; or, following a generation of influence, their own missions reverted to business as usual, or to some other agenda. Furthermore, mission history reveals extended periods in which little (or no) critique was done; tragedies like the Crusades and Colonialism resulted.

Church growth, however, has contributed such a substantial strategic perspective to the minds of informed mission leaders that the situation may now be permanently altered for the better. This suggestion can be confirmed by perusing a recent edition of *Perspectives on the World Christian Movement*.[13] This collection, now almost eight hundred pages, contains 124 articles divided into four sections: the Biblical Perspective, the Historical Perspective, the Cultural Perspective, and the Strategic Perspective. The number of articles in the Strategic Perspective section now equals the number in any two of the other three sections.

One cannot account for such attention to mission strategy in mission today apart from the paradigm-level influence of church growth thought. McGavran taught missional churches to love the Lord of the Harvest with their minds as well as their hearts; we have experienced a quiet revolution in the minds of many people who are devoted to Christian mission. Many mission leaders today devote enormously more attention than their predecessors to strategic questions like the following:

1. What is our essential *mission*, our main business, our driving purpose?

2. Within this mission, what are our *objectives*, and our priorities within those objectives?

3. What are the core values, beliefs, convictions, experiences, and stories that define our *identity*?

---

13. Ralph W. Winter and Steven C. Hawthorne, eds., *Perspectives on the World Christian Movement* (Pasadena, CA: William Carey Library, 1999).

4. To, and with, what *people* are we in mission?

5. What *cultural* patterns have shaped them, and how do we relate to those patterns?

6. What *religious* worldview(s) and experiences have shaped them, and how do we respond to those influences?

7. What else must we know about the *context* for mission?

8. What *approaches*, ministries, and methods will effectively serve and reach them?

9. How shall we *organize* for mission? Who makes strategic decisions? What policies will advance, rather than frustrate, this mission?

10. What *personnel* do we need to deploy in mission? What physical resources do they need? Where are the sources for the needed human and financial resources?

As missions mature, mission leaders have often addressed other often ignored but indispensable strategic questions, like:

11. How do we monitor progress, *evaluate* our mission, and make mid-course corrections?

12. How has the *context changed* since we last evaluated our mission?

13. What approaches, programs, and ministries are no longer productive and should be jettisoned, thereby freeing time and resources for more productive action?

14. When, and how, do we turn over the mission, churches, and ministries to the nationals?

15. How will *relationships* between the sending church, the mission, and the younger church be defined?

16. How shall the younger church plan for reaching and serving more populations in its society, and for its future mission to other peoples?

Those questions, of course, are not exhaustive, and each question is an umbrella for more specific questions. Though the more general "management revolution" once catalyzed by Peter Drucker to understand organizations and leadership has influenced many mission leaders, McGavran and his colleagues advanced specific principles of strategic mission. More important, research has explored the range of options available within each major question and has suggested which options are more usually effective. (Reflecting within the generic questions, for example, "How shall we *organize* for mission?" and "Who makes strategic decisions?" research has demonstrated that decentralized mission organizations are usually more effective than centralized mission organizations, and strategic decisions made by field leaders are usually more effective than strategic decisions made at headquarters.)

A Research Tradition in Early Adolescence

Within the two issues of effective evangelism and mission strategy, the church growth school has made its most enduring contribution. Of course, it would be fatuous to assume we had "answered" the strategic questions and could now "move on" to other matters. Church growth's achievement, to date, is not at all in the same league with the "pure sciences," which are now so close to mapping the universe, and the human brain, and the human genetic code, and to achieving so many other long-standing goals that some science writers

147

now predict "the end of science"; one day, they forecast, scientists may have few remaining unanswered major questions on their plate!

Church growth, with the more general study of mission, is not even in the same league as the behavioral sciences, whose leaders may acknowledge that their fields are in early adolescence. Behavioral scientists have discovered many specific insights, but they have fathomed few of their big questions deeply. Most of their big discoveries still wait; many of their important issues, already identified, will challenge researchers for generations to come, but the emergence of an overarching macro-theory about human behavior in society and culture is nowhere in sight. Likewise, one day, through continued field research and reflection with other disciplines, we will know enormously more about effective missional Christianity than we know now, but that day is nowhere in sight.

So, church growth people have no compelling reason to shift from strategy to theology as our main business. *Nevertheless*, we are told that we have contributed, at the level of specific insights, to the Christian movement's theological understanding. Some of our insights about Christian conversion and Christian experience were suggested, above, in the list of church growth's discoveries about effective evangelism. The important role of public Christian ethical teaching was featured in the second chapter. One chapter does not permit a complete report on church growth's modest theological contribution, but contributions in five areas of Christian thought are worth noting.

Five Contributions to Theology

1. An Appraisal of "New Theologies"

We believe that our field observation has demonstrated that most of the entrants in the lengthy parade of "new theologies," from Friedrich Schleiermacher's nineteenth-century innovations to present-day projects, have lacked the demonstrated power to inform significant enduring Christian movements among their pre-Christian populations. (One reason is because virtually each new theology has a short shelf life.) Some new theologies enable the church to keep some of our people in some of our churches, for perhaps a generation, but they have not informed and sustained many outreach movements. (Indeed, some theologians argue that evangelism, in any form, should not even be done!) The available field data suggest that the theology that usually scripts an actual Christian movement is that tradition's meaningful interpretation of classical Christianity for the context.

Two apparent exceptions come to mind. First, a publicly magnetic Christian leader comes along periodically, and attracts some followers and some press; but, since we cannot clone such personalities, no wider sustaining Christian movement results. Second, we have observed the proliferation of "Prosperity Gospel" churches in many nations; however, since their major premise is that you *can* "serve both God and mammon," they may not sufficiently qualify for the "Christian" part of a Christian movement.

2. Contribution to the Doctrine of Creation

Christianity's doctrine of *creation* affirmed that God created everything "good" and, although creation is negatively impacted by humanity's sin and fall, God's creation remains good and will still be used in the work of redemption; we dramatize this truth every time we baptize with water and every time we offer the bread that represents the Bread of Life.

McGavran saw humanity as "a marvelous mosaic" of thousands of distinct tongues and cultures. Charles Van Engen reminds us of McGavran's once-revolutionary insight: that God's good creation includes *human cultures*, and this "includes the socio-cultural, linguistic and world-view particularities of each people group."[14] Furthermore, a given culture's worldview functions like a refracting lens—affecting the way the people perceive and receive the gospel. We are, therefore, to study the earth's cultures, to discover the "indigenous" ways to communicate the gospel's meaning within their culture. Any culture, McGavran was confident, will provide points of contact for communicating the gospel.

McGavran also perceived that God's gracious involvement with creation, in all of its fallenness, brokenness, and chaos, is always prompting receptivity in the lives of some people, and peoples. Van Engen explains that McGavran and his colleagues, "without blaming God" for all of the momentous and tragic events in history, "found that political unrest, willing or forced migration, movement of peoples from predominantly rural areas to the city, natural disasters, and even wars seemed to create new openness among people groups to be willing to consider the Christian church's communication of the Gospel in word and deed."[15]

3. Contribution to the Doctrine of Human Nature

The church growth field has contributed to the church's doctrine of human nature. Western theologians, scripted by the paradigm of Western individualism, have generally perceived all humanity as a vast aggregation of billions of individuals who matter to God. Church growth people, schooled in cultural anthropology and reading in Matthew 28 that Christ commissioned the church to go and make disciples among *panta ta ethne*, have substantially recovered the understanding of the scriptures (and of most of the world's cultures) that most people have such a corporate identity that we are

14. Charles Van Engen, "Theological Foundations of Bridges of God: The Mission Theology Legacy of Donald Anderson McGavran" (delivered to the annual meeting of the American Society for Church Growth, November 11, 2005), 6–7.

15. Van Engen, "Theological Foundations of Bridges of God," 10.

commissioned to target the affinity groups that shape their people's identity, worldview, and decisions. The church growth school has taught much of the church to view humanity not as "atoms," but as "molecules"—the clans, tribes, castes, peer groups, and other affinity groups who process new possibilities, and reach important decisions, more or less together.

Church growth reflection upon the biblical metaphor of the "harvest" has produced significant insight into human nature. Prior to church growth, much of Protestant Christianity was divided between the Calvinist-Reformed tradition and the Wesleyan-Arminian tradition. John Calvin's logical mind had framed the debate and reached one rational conclusion. The doctrine of the sovereignty of God was the major premise of his theological system. He had also experienced God's grace as an "irresistible" force. Yet he observed some of Geneva's people clearly resisting the "irresistible" grace of a "sovereign" God. Rigorous logic led him to conclude, from those premises, that the resisters were created without the capacity to perceive and respond to grace (i.e., they were not among the "Elect").

Calvin, however, may have functioned like a photographer who assumed that his photographic subjects have always looked like they did at the time he took the photograph, and they always will. John Wesley distanced himself from Calvin's doctrine of "double election," because of what he believed that the biblical revelation teaches about the love of God for all people, *and* because he observed many of eighteenth-century England's people, and whole communities, changing over time. Wesley anticipated Donald McGavran's observations about volatile human *receptivity*:

> Fluctuating receptivity is a most prominent aspect of human nature and society.... The receptivity or responsiveness of individuals waxes and wanes. No person is equally ready at all times to follow the way.... Peoples and societies also vary in responsiveness. Whole segments of mankind resist the gospel for periods—often very long

periods—and then ripen to the good news....Missions in Asia, Africa, and Latin America also abundantly illustrate the fact that societies ripen to the gospel at different times.... Sudden ripenings, far from being unusual, are common.... One thing is clear—receptivity wanes as often as it waxes. Like the tide, it comes in and goes out. Unlike the tide, no one can guarantee when it goes out that it will soon come back again.[16]

McGavran's longtime colleague at Fuller's School of World Mission, Arthur Glasser, reported that, with such insights, "We feel we have leaped over the inscrutable mystery that down through the years has provoked endless theological debate and ecclesiastical division."[17] Church growth reflection has, at least for some people, substantially *resolved* a long-standing theological debate.

4. Contribution to Understanding the Gospel

It involves no stretch to report that church growth people have also advanced Christianity's understanding of *the gospel*. Some theologians appear confused about the difference between the gospel and theology, or they use the two terms so interchangeably that, in the writings of one theologian or another, virtually any doctrine (or point of view) is included within, or *is*, "the gospel."

Our experience in mission with pre-Christian populations, however, has led to a more careful distinction. Consistent with Anselm's definition of theology as "faith seeking understanding," the term *gospel* refers to the message within the wider body of theology that makes initial faith possible. So, in outreach to pre-Christian people, we labor to clarify "what they need to know" from theology's treasure to make faith a possibility for them.

16. Donald McGavran, *Understanding Church Growth* (Grand Rapids: Eerdmans, 1980), 245–48.
17. Quoted in Harvey M. Conn, *Theological Perspectives on Church Growth* (Den Dulk Foundation, 1976), 145.

Our experience in mission also teaches us that the gospel can, and should, be communicated in many different ways—such as story and analogy, music and drama, poetry and fiction, folk arts and fine arts, and conversation and testimony, as well as through preaching and teaching. Mission experience also teaches us that the gospel's meaning is often communicated nonverbally. When, for instance, first-century Galileans observed Jesus and the disciples in ministry to the very groups of people (such as lepers and harlots, and blind, deaf, and possessed people, and zealots and tax collectors) who were excluded from the temple, that ministry "spoke" volumes. The non-verbal communication was not completely nonverbal, however; audience members conversed among (and within) themselves to construct their meaning of an event.

Furthermore, since virtually no one "gets" and lives by (say) the message of grace with their first exposure to the message, its communication typically takes place many times, in many ways, over time, before people adopt it. And since the gospel is not one theme, but many, much communication is needed over time.

Some theologians, however, may not perceive a gospel of many themes. Some theologians, without mission experience, may reduce their understanding of the gospel to one essential theme. So often, according to one theologian or another, Christianity's gospel is almost *only* about grace, or the love of God, or the kingdom of God, or justification, or sanctification, or liberation.

It may take actual experience in mission to blast some theologians into a larger understanding. In one case, a Lutheran theologian served for years as a missionary in West Africa. As a Lutheran, he preached justification almost every Sunday. The church grew, and for his doctoral thesis he surveyed converts to determine what themes in Christianity's message had engaged them. Few converts referred to justification. Most of them responded to the good news that Jesus Christ can set us free from the powers of evil. The missionary could not recall many times that he had ever preached on that theme, but *Christus Victor* was a prominent theme in the church's liturgy. As the people discovered the gospel of the power of Christ through the liturgy, and from people's testimonies, and through many conversations and prayers, the church grew.

Bluntly stated, many mission scholars are convinced of a bigger and more comprehensive gospel than many theologians have yet discovered. While no analogy is adequate to the gospel, in one book[18] I feature the gospel as a diamond, a multifaceted gem. While Jesus himself primarily proclaimed and taught about the promised kingdom (or reign) of God that was now breaking into history as he forgave sins, healed diseases, cast out demons, and preached as one having authority, following Jesus's execution and resurrection and the gift of his Spirit at Pentecost, the gospel's meaning expanded enormously.

From the gospel of Jesus that focused essentially on the kingdom of God, his movement's gospel about Jesus Christ now took on many themes. The church now explicitly proclaimed what had been more implicit in Jesus's teaching and ministry—that Jesus was (and is) Israel's promised Messiah. "Jesus is Lord" emerged as the movement's first creedal affirmation. The symbol of the fish caught on early and widely, as well as the symbol of the cross. His followers believed he was the supreme revelation of God and of what humans were meant to be. No one theme could now communicate the larger gospel's full meaning, so the gospel became like a mosaic of truth claims, or a gem with many different facets. It became, for instance, good news about the grace of God, and the righteousness of God, and the love of God, and the peace of God and the restoration of the image of God in people who turned to God. It became a gospel of the forgiveness of sins and new birth, reconciliation and redemption,

---

18. See George G. Hunter III, *Christian, Evangelical and...Democrat?* (Nashville: Abingdon Press, 2006), 10–12.

justification and salvation and sanctification, abundant life and eternal life, a new covenant and a new community and a new humanity, a new heaven and a new earth.

The gospel gem includes, as one prominent facet, the good news that Christ's death and resurrection have defeated the power of death (humanity's final enemy) and that Christ has preceded us in heaven to prepare a place for us. However, in contrast to the ancient mystery religions and Gnostic religions (as should be clear from the multiple themes in the last paragraph), Christianity is not only about going to heaven—though, today, many people assume it is only about that, or almost so. (Nineteenth-century Holiness evangelists used to remind their people that even this part of the gospel was not about "gitting" us to heaven, but about "fitting" us for heaven.) Finally, Jesus's own leading edge of the gospel that emphasized the kingdom of God has remained a large, bright, and central piece of the gospel mosaic through much of Christian history.

The gospel we know in scripture is, however, much more than a sum total of themes. The gospel is rooted in *historical events*, most notably the liberation of the Hebrew people from slavery in Egypt and the resurrection of Jesus of Nazareth from death. Without the exodus, there would be no Judaism; without the exodus and the resurrection, there would be no Christianity.

The gospel is also rooted in the *experiences* of the people of God. Following their exodus from Egypt, the Hebrew people experienced the God of Abraham with them, as a cloud by day and a pillar of fire by night; the disciples lived with Jesus and observed his ministries and miracles, and following his resurrection, their hearts burned within them as he walked with them and opened the scriptures to them.

The gospel is also *narrative*. All four Gospel writers report many of the stories that Jesus told, and they tell the story of what God was up to in the Christ Event; that story is the center in the grand narrative that begins with creation and tells the long story of Israel and the early history of the New Israel, and ends with the promise that God's kingdom will be consummated.

Finally, the gospel is also a *perspective*. Christianity's truth claims are given not merely that we might believe them, but that we can perceive life and the world through the lenses of New Testament faith. (C. S. Lewis once suggested that we don't need more books about Christianity as much as we need more books about other things from a Christian perspective.)

5. Contribution to Understanding the Church's Importance

Church growth's contribution to the doctrine of the church has been significant for many Protestants. Among Protestant evangelicals, church growth people were once somewhat unusual for taking the church seriously, for having a "high" doctrine of the church, or for even *having* a doctrine of the church! (Some Protestants still assume that the church is more or less optional.) Moreover, church growth people stand among the probable minority of Protestants who affirm St. Augustine's conclusion, "There is no salvation outside the church." Our reasons may contrast with Augustine's; we simply observe that virtually no one experiences grace and second birth and new life, and becomes a disciple, apart from communities of faith. We believe with John Wesley that "Christianity is not a solitary religion." Involvement in the body of Christ is essential. Indeed, many people experience "belonging" before they experience "believing."[19]

Nevertheless, church growth people often critique churches and denominations. We believe that churches were meant to be more like local Christian movements than inward, diocesan, local institutions.

---

19. See chapter 4 of my *Celtic Way of Evangelism,* rev. ed. (Nashville: Abingdon Press, 2010) for some of the history and nuances of the "belonging before believing" principle.

And we believe that local Christian movements were meant to live even more for pre-Christian people than for church members.[20]

Furthermore, we take the empirical church seriously; we actually study churches, and movements of churches, warts and all; and that data, supplementing biblical and theological data, helps shape and nuance our understanding of the body of Christ. Many theologies of the church, from the pens of desk theologians, discuss the church as a theoretical abstraction, removed from reference to actual churches! My *Leading and Managing a Growing Church* demonstrated that the church is, after all, a human organization—requiring leadership and management somewhat like any organization, but a unique human organization:

> Some church leaders resist insights from the literatures of leadership, management, and organization effectiveness because, they say, that the Church is *different*. The church isn't an organization; it is an Organism—the Body of Christ. Christ is its head, He is the Leader, and we are called to run the church on *spiritual* principles, not the principles of Madison Avenue and the corporate world.
>
> This "spiritual" perspective on the Church does contain a crucial perspective on this matter. The Church is, or should be, different from McDonalds, Sears, Rotary, GM, IBM, MIT, and P&G. Ignoring the fact that each of those seven organization are very different from the other six, five things (at least) do make the Church a different kind of organization: 1) The Church has a distinct Source. Christ built it, on the rock of faith in Him as Messiah and risen Lord, to be the New Israel, the Body of Christ, and the extension of His incarnation. 2) From the ancient apostles, the Church has a distinct message—the gospel and the fuller biblical revelation. . . . 3) The Church has a distinct Purpose—to reach the peoples of the earth, to help them become reconciled to God, liberated from their sins, restored to God's purpose, and deployed in God's wider mission seeking health, peace, justice, and salvation for all people and (some would add) all creation. 4) Through such sources as the Ten

20. I have discussed, at some length, what we think we know about movemental Christianity and its leadership in *The Recovery of a Contagious Methodist Movement* (Nashville: Abingdon, 2011), especially in the second chapter.

Commandments, the Sermon on the Mount, and the Great Commandment to love God and neighbor, the Church is given the Ethic that should limit, shape, and focus how Christians do Kingdom business. 5) As "No one can say 'Jesus is Lord' except by the Holy Spirit," not much else that is supremely important in our total mission is likely to succeed without Third Person power behind, attending, and blessing our efforts.

Though the Church is a different kind of organization, however, it is still an organization. In common with other organizations, the Church is an interdependent aggregation of people with some shared history, identity, and culture, who pull together in coordinated activities to achieve the organization's objectives. Granting its distinctive source, message, mission, ethic, and reliance, churches nevertheless have much in common with other organizations, particularly other voluntary organizations. When churches achieve their objectives, many of the reasons are the same as when other kinds of organizations achieve their objectives. If it helps to know, much of the best literature on leadership and management is written by devoted Christians, such as Peter Drucker and Ken Blanchard. Nevertheless, there is no "Christian" body of management theory any more than there is a "Christian" grammar, or a "Christian" arithmetic, or a "Christian" chemistry, or a "Christian" way to train for the decathlon. Presumably, Christians who are effectively in the world (while no longer of it) will connect subjects and predicates, or calculate the square root of a number, or measure and mix a solution, or prepare for a shot put competition more or less like anyone else.

Occasionally, I meet church leaders who deny all of this. I have concluded, reluctantly, that they may be "heretics"—harboring a *Docetic Ecclesiology!* That glib charge warrants an explanation! In the first centuries of Christianity, some Christians were influenced by a Greek philosophy called Gnosticism. Gnostic believed that matter, and particularly the human body, are Evil. Gnostic Christians believed, therefore, that in the Incarnation God did not really take on human flesh, and He could not possibly have suffered on the cross; he only appeared to be human, and he only appeared to suffer, like an actor playing a role in a salvation drama. FitzSimons Allison, in *The Cruelty of Heresy: An Affirmation of Christian Orthodoxy*[21]

---

21.   (New York: Morehouse Publishing, 1994), 27–28.

explains their view and their label: "The Docetists found it incomprehensible that Jesus could have actually suffered. They answered the essential questions about him by insisting that he only *appeared* to suffer, to weep, to thirst, to hunger, to sweat in agony, and to die, and that his incarnate human state was so spiritual that he only appeared to be human. (Docetism is derived from the word *dokein*, which means 'to seem, to appear.')"[22]

The Council of Nicea branded this view a serious heresy, and affirmed that Jesus Christ was indeed "made man," "was crucified," "suffered and was buried." The Council insisted that Jesus took on our full humanity because, in the words of ancient theologians—"What he did not assume, he could not save," and, "He became as we are, that we might become like Him."

Docetism is still with us, in several forms, but "docetic ecclesiology" may be a new form. As the old Docetism claimed that Jesus's body was not a real human body, though it appeared to be, **docetic ecclesiology maintains that the church, the body of Christ, is not a real human organization, though it appears to be.** An orthodox doctrine of the church, however, would affirm the church's full humanity. As Jesus's body was a real human body—as any physician checking for a pulse or blood pressure could have affirmed, so the body of Christ is a real human organization—reflecting many of the same dynamics, and managed by many of the same principles, we find in other organizations. The church, because of its distinct source, message, mission, ethic, and reliance, is a different kind of organization than Honda or Harvard, but an organization nevertheless. The most effective Christian leaders will be informed both by what we know about organizations and by what we know about churches.

22. George G. Hunter III, *Leading & Managing a Growing Church* (Nashville: Abingdon Press, 2000), 21–24.

Why the Church Is Part of the Good News

I have discovered some churches across the land whose people do reach out and invite. Somewhat like the ancient apostles and their churches, these more "apostolic congregations" target pre-Christian populations and they regard reaching and serving them as their main business. Several of my books[23] contend (in part) that churches featuring cultural relevance, small groups, lay ministries, outreach ministries, and involvement in world mission thereby build people who are enormously more likely to engage in apostolic ministry than the demographically similar members of the traditional church down the street.

These churches often make a difference. Plant a faithful church with an outward focus in almost any community on earth, and you may find that crime decreases, literacy increases, children are immunized, addicts find the path to recovery, families and schools are supported, musicians and artists express their gifts, people experience dignity and healthier self-esteem, and they face the future with less despair and more hope, and much more.

In the late 1960s, while I pastored a West Indies immigrant church in Birmingham, England, our circuit's lay leader told a story that reminded me of why churches are so indispensable.

The Egg Growers Association of England was holding its annual convention in London. For six years, most of England's poultry population had feasted on a new scientifically supplemented chicken feed.

---

23. See George G. Hunter III, *Church for the Unchurched* (Nashville: Abingdon, 1996), *Radical Outreach: The Recovery of Apostolic Ministry and Evangelism* (Nashville: Abingdon, 2003), *The Apostolic Congregation: Church Growth Reconceived for a New Generation* (Nashville: Abingdon, 2009), and *Should We Change Our Game Plan?* (Nashville: Abingdon, 2013).

The association's chief scientist presented his annual report. He reported "some good news and some bad news." The good news was that egg production per hen had more than tripled and, as the hens were now experiencing genetic changes, in several generations they would be producing ten to twenty eggs per day. That was the good news.

"The bad news," he reported, "is that supply of eggs will vastly exceed the demand for eggs. We know of no marketing strategy that can increase nearly enough demand for the eggs that will be produced. If anticipated trends continue, in ten to twelve years, all of England will be knee-deep in eggs."

The scientist requested the afternoon off to field-test a possible solution. He hailed a taxi to Westminster Abbey and asked to see the dean.

"Dean, I understand you have a campaign to raise twenty million pounds to restore the foundations of Westminster."

"Yes," the head priest responded, "we have such a campaign, we are behind schedule, and I fear for the future of England's most beloved church."

The scientist inched toward his proposal. "In your services, don't you have a prayer that says, 'Give us this day our daily bread'?"

"Yes," said the priest, "we have such a prayer. It is our most ancient prayer."

The scientist moved in. "I represent an organization that will give the Abbey the twenty million pounds, in installments as you need it, if you will do one thing for us.

The senior priest leaned forward. "What is it you want from us?"

"Beginning this Sunday, just eliminate the word 'bread' and substitute the word 'eggs.'"

You have sensed the plot that the scientist wanted to "hatch." Westminster Abbey was the trend-setting church. If the Abbey started this revised version of the Lord's Prayer, England's other churches would too, the new version would be taught in schools, and soon the nation would pray daily for eggs!

When the priest understood the scientist's proposal, however, he threw him out of his office.

The scientist returned to the convention and, that evening, completed his presentation. He reported that if the nation prayed for eggs the association's problem would have been solved. "However, the priest said no and he threw me out."

He added, "It makes you wonder how much the bread companies are paying him, doesn't it?"

I am amused by the joke's punch line, because of the assumption behind it. No one does anything, except for what they will get out of it. Self-interest drives the world.

Christians believe that, in the church, God raised up an alternative community with an alternative life and lifestyle. We are the people who are committed (in the spirit of 2 Corinthians 5:15) to "live no more for ourselves" but for others and "for the one who died for them and was raised."

That is one big reason why churches can be very good news.

Index

CPSIA information can be obtained
at www.ICGtesting.com
Printed in the USA
LVOW04s0609110117

520493LV00001BA/1/P